praise for
one long listening

"*one long listening* is a lyric wonder, a joyful wandering, an ode to unknowing, a love letter to a friend, a still pool of grief, a fuzzy sock, a dancing crane. That a memoir can be all of these things and more is a testament to its author's boundless curiosity. Chenxing Han beautifully channels Simone Weil's definition of prayer as 'absolutely unmixed attention.' She embraces misspellings, mishearings, and misunderstandings as pathways toward connection, while offering a fresh counterpoint to misrepresentations of hospital chaplaincy and American Buddhism. We need more books like this: a tender and patient act of care."

SIMON HAN, author of
Nights When Nothing Happened

"Written with the delicate ellipsis of Chinese poetry and a novelist's eye for telling detail, Chenxing Han's *one long listening* is an engaging collage of unforgettable vignettes that meander through her years of hospital chaplaincy, Buddhist studies, world travel, and the heartbreaking loss of her young best friend. Born in Shanghai, raised in America, Han offers honest and poignant stories about cultural displacement—a great challenge of our time—that will charm and unsettle you."

NORMAN FISCHER, Zen priest, poet, and author of
When You Greet Me I Bow

"Reading *one long listening* is like walking through a rainbow of light and tears: luminous, transparent, mysterious, and moving, Chenxing Han's exquisite memoir is an immersive exploration of the grit and grief of life interwoven with the boundless glories of the spirit."

CATHERINE CHUNG, author of *The Tenth Muse*

"*one long listening* is a beautifully written, thoughtful, and thoroughly honest journey through loneliness, grief, and fulfillment. It is a book that resonates deeply, both emotionally and on a literary level, as a sentence-by-sentence pleasure whose distinctive structure distills each chapter down to a powerful essence."

JAY CASPIAN KANG, *New Yorker* staff writer and author of *The Loneliest Americans*

"*one long listening* is Chenxing Han's journey through East and West, life and death, resiliency and vulnerability. It is written like Thomas Merton's classic *Conjectures of a Guilty Bystander*, but from the perspective of engagement. In *one long listening*, Chaplain Han actually shares what she heard: amplify the compassion, remember to try and taste the many flavors of this world, and refresh our stories. This book will inspire you to listen very deeply."

PAMELA AYO YETUNDE, ThD, chaplain, pastoral counselor, and author of *Casting Indra's Net*

"Chenxing Han is a deft guide through the interstices of the heart. Honesty conditions the ever-shifting ground. Insight fuels the flowing movement. Intimacy colors the undulating landscape. Joining her journey into a sublime realm at the core of our humanity, wayseekers are invited to feast on the marrow of life."

PAULA ARAI, PhD, author of *Painting Enlightenment*

"In a world living in a sea of grief, this expression from our dear sister in spirit is a blessed gift for the heart and mind of all. Please benefit from this beautiful healing balm."

DR. PEGGY ROWE WARD and DR. LARRY WARD, coauthors of *Love's Garden*

"Chenxing Han's luminous spiritual practice of friendship, as the Buddha said, is not 'half of the holy life—it is the whole of it.' Her journey as a Buddhist chaplain is grounded, unmade, regrounded by an immense understanding of her relations with other humans and nonhumans as instances of companionship, transient yet eternal in its recurring resonance. Each meeting unfurls with tenderness, intimacy, generosity. This sustained climate of sacred concordance—with friends, strangers, patients, teachers, winds, birds, trees—is a flower nourished by, as Han writes, one long listening. In a world deprived of listening and overfilled with pain and grief, Han's habit of listening is a habit of love.

"Han's writing, like her presence, is a radiant stream of wakeful, loving life. She plays with multiple layers of language, translation, legibility, and karmic force as she listens to the poetry, calamity, comedy, and mystery of life unfolding. The dreamlike vignettes of her own and others' moments of despair and delight, sickness and stability, flow like a vast river, with no beginning, no end, now terribly agitated, now exquisitely calm. Reader: Exhale deeply, empty yourself to listen to Han listening. Watch how bodily and psychic pains could turn into smiles in this magic river of long, long listening."

QUYÊN NGUYỄN-HOÀNG,
translator of *Chronicles of a Village*
by Nguyễn Thanh Hiện

one
long
listening

one
long
listening

a memoir of grief,
friendship, and spiritual care

Chenxing Han

North Atlantic Books
Huichin, unceded Ohlone land
aka Berkeley, California

Published by
North Atlantic Books
Huichin, unceded Ohlone land
aka Berkeley, California

Cover art © gettyimages.com/venimo
Cover design by Jess Morphew
Book design by Happenstance Type-O-Rama

Printed in the United States of America

one long listening: a memoir of grief, friendship, and spiritual care is sponsored and published by North Atlantic Books, an educational nonprofit based in the unceded Ohlone land Huichin (*aka* Berkeley, CA) that collaborates with partners to develop cross-cultural perspectives, nurture holistic views of art, science, the humanities, and healing, and seed personal and global transformation by publishing work on the relationship of body, spirit, and nature.

North Atlantic Books' publications are distributed to the US trade and internationally by Penguin Random House Publisher Services. For further information, visit our website at www.northatlantic-books.com.

Library of Congress Cataloging-in-Publication Data

Names: Han, Chenxing, 1986- author.
Title: One long listening : a meditation on Buddhist chaplaincy, grief, and
    spiritual friendship / Chenxing Han.
Description: Berkeley : North Atlantic Books, 2023. | Summary: "Chenxing
    Han writes prose surrounding her experiences through love and loss as a
    Buddhist immigrant. This book examines what we give to others and how we
    give back to ourselves"— Provided by publisher.
Identifiers: LCCN 2022018710 (print) | LCCN 2022018711 (ebook) | ISBN
    9781623177850 (trade paperback) | ISBN 9781623177867 (ebook)
Subjects: LCSH: Han, Chenxing, 1986- author. | Meditation—Buddhism. |
    Buddhism—Doctrines. | Thought and thinking—Religious
    aspects—Buddhism. | Consciousness--Religious aspects—Buddhism.
Classification: LCC BQ5612 .H356 2023 (print) | LCC BQ5612 (ebook) | DDC
    294.3/4432—dc23/eng/20220825
LC record available at https://lccn.loc.gov/2022018710
LC ebook record available at https://lccn.loc.gov/2022018711

1 2 3 4 5 6 7 8 9 KPC 28 27 26 25 24 23

This book includes recycled material and material from well-managed forests. North Atlantic Books is committed to the protection of our environment. We print on recycled paper whenever possible and partner with printers who strive to use environmentally responsible practices.

for amy and the hummingbirds

table of contents

gratitude

ally stewart
for planting the seed

my cpe supervisors—carrie buckner, va' nechia rayford,
lavera crawley—& peers
for entering the thicket

the hospital staff & patients & their families
for braving the wilds

drs. wei-jen teng 鄧偉仁 & aries gu 辜琛瑜
for opening the mountain

rev. dr. seigen yamaoka
for sowing the breeze

gillian hamel, tim mckee, emily shapiro & everyone at
north atlantic books
for nurturing the leaves

quyên nguyễn-hoàng, neekaan oshidary, trinh luu,
elaine lai & nancy chu
for shaping the grove

anning ye 叶安宁
for translating the trees

dawn kwan
for illuminating the canopy

angi ye 叶安琪 & xiaoping han 韩小平
for establishing our roots

trent walker
for embracing the mossy forest

alex winn
for traversing the thorny-sublime trails

lynn & jon & mark (& dave & kirsten & katie) frohnmayer
for being the sun the rain the sky the stars

amy elizabeth frohnmayer winn
for beaming still with your boundless love

bridge

The summer before she died, I visited the Musée Guimet for the first time.

By then, the young woman who was once my college roommate had been diagnosed with acute myeloid leukemia. She was twenty-nine. Like her two sisters, complications from the rare genetic disease Fanconi anemia would take her from this world.

The largest collection of Asian art outside Asia sweeps all thoughts of FA and AML from my mind. In the museum's central atrium, I encounter Khmer sculptures so exquisite my chest aches. To stand in that pristine hall where the air is temperature-controlled to a T, I had flown from Phnom Penh to Bangkok to Dubai to London, arriving in Paris by train. In Phnom Penh, I lived just around the corner from the National Museum of Cambodia, where pigeons meandered underfoot, bird poop graffitied the walls, and chickens clucked at ancient statuary. From the central courtyard, an occasional sultry breeze stirred human and avian visitors alike as we roamed inside the National Museum's open-air pavilions.

Standing in that pristine and breezeless hall on the ground level of the Guimet, I ache for the Khmer sculptures there in the 16th arrondissement of Paris, so far from home.

Homesickness and friendsickness. Twin aches accompany my ascent to the museum dome. Up and up I go, tracing the spine of the uncoiling naga of a staircase.

Here is what I can tell you about the structure of this memoir. I met it in the rotunda of the Guimet that day: eight thousand strips of tiger bamboo, held together by nothing more than air and weave. A six-tusked elephant spills from ceiling to floor, a tangle of roots cascades from trunk to earth, an ephemeral installation by fourth-generation bamboo artist Shouchiku Tanabe. Tanabe treats each tawny strip as if it were the whole, lets the bamboo breathe itself into being. Empty of form, formed of emptiness, the structure has no beginning or end. Fluid as a river, sure as one too, it evaporates all distinctions between past and future, sickness and health, life and death.

That domed room, free from birth and extinction, tarnish and purity, boon and loss . . . it was unbearable to leave.

But one cannot live in rotundas forever. I descended the naga staircase. Time resumed. Her cancer kept spreading, undeterred by the chemo, the radiation, the bone marrow transplant. Back in Phnom Penh, I couldn't get the Bon Iver song "Woods" out of my mind. *I'm up in the woods—I'm down on my mind—I'm building a still—To slow down the time.*

This book is that still, a mala bracelet of rumination-worn beads.

In the beads that follow, proper names are largely absent. My reasons for this choice are twofold: to protect people's privacy, and to honor the Asian cultures that have formed me.

胖阿姨 and 瘦阿姨 are not reducible to their chubbiness or skinniness. When I call these aunties by their paired nicknames, I celebrate the friendship that gave rise to their playful monikers. We do not call each other by our full names. The omission endears us to each other.

កើត រ័ន is among the Khmer Dharma song masters whose teachings resculpted the trajectory of my partner's life. Greeting me for the first time at her home in the Cambodian countryside, she cradles my face between her palms and calls me កូន. I call this revered teacher and blind grandmother អ្នកគ្រូ and លោកយាយ. I would never address her as Koet Ran. The omission bespeaks respect.

As in the two paragraphs above, virtually all of the Chinese, Khmer, and other Asian scripts in this book are translated in context. The unglossary on page 267 relays the *pīnyīn* for the Chinese characters along with phonetic transcriptions for words in Thai, Khmer, and Japanese.

Why such an oblique and incomplete method of translation? I wanted to convey, in this mala of a memoir, not only what chaplains *do,* but how chaplaincy *feels.* Choosing honesty over ease, I let the frustrations and opacities remain. I hope you'll indulge me this choice, in the Buddhist spirit of 不知最親切. *Not knowing is most intimate.*

The beads ahead do not conform to linear time. They circle, primarily, around three autumns of my life. In the fall of 2014, I began a yearlong chaplaincy residency program in California. In the fall of 2015, I moved to Taiwan to spend a semester at a Buddhist college. In the fall of 2016, I was undone by a dear friend's too-soon death.

I've heard it said that there are as many ways to do chaplaincy as there are chaplains. This book is about one chaplain's way.

PART I
一期一會

ichi-go ichi-e

NEAR THE END OF MY yearlong residency in hospital chaplaincy, I buy a one-way ticket to Taiwan.

My parents, who are both computer engineers, are not amused. They warn me about the dire state of the Taiwanese economy (Mom) and suggest a "total career reboot" (Dad). Alarmed that I am nearing thirty with nary a job prospect in sight, they ask, "Why are you going to a Buddhist monastery?" And, also: "Why are you throwing away your future?"

The second question seems a bit loaded, so I mumble a response to the first. I'm trying to understand chaplaincy outside the Christian-dominated American context. I want to see how a Taiwanese Buddhist institute teaches spiritual care.

But here's a more honest response. I read somewhere that you go to the monastery to find out why you are going to the monastery.

Which is to say, I don't know.

SURELY MY EDUCATION—NURSERY IN SHANGHAI, Little Ducklings day care in Pittsburgh, public schools in Pennsylvania and Washington state, undergrad and grad programs in California—has amounted to more than *I don't know?*

My parents are not mollified. Have I considered becoming a product manager? And, implicitly: What kind of immigrant daughter goes *back* to the country* her parents struggled so hard to leave in the first place?

To be fair, they aren't the only ones perplexed. For those who have never heard of chaplaincy,[†] it can be discomfiting to meet a hospital employee who does not fit the familiar categories—doctor, nurse, social worker, occupational therapist, phlebotomist. For example: At my mom's annual music party the summer before I steal away to Taiwan, her coworker corners me in the kitchen. Interrogating me about my job, he works himself into a paroxysm of bewilderment. *But what is it that you* do*?!* he wails, throwing up his hands as the refrigerator spits ice cubes down my back.

When people at the hospital ask, *Why does my father have cancer, Is grandma ever gonna leave the ICU, Where is my daughter now that she's dead,* my response is the brokenest of records.

I don't know, I don't know, I don't know.

---

* Technically they left mainland China and not Taiwan, but never mind PRC–ROC relations; the point (project management's superiority over Buddhist chaplaincy, the ingratitude of immigrant children) still stands.

† A category I fit into for the first two decades of my life

SOMETHING ELSE I DON'T KNOW: Why, at the base of the mountain crowned by the Taiwanese Buddhist monastery, there is a phalanx of cars parked along a two-lane road that sees little traffic otherwise.

On the mountain, after our Topics in Holistic Education class one day, a nun catches me squinting in the direction of the cars.

"The dead outnumber the living here," she observes.

"Oh . . . ?" I venture, intrigued.

Crow's feet sprout behind horn-rimmed frames.

"This rural town is a popular place for grave sites," the nun informs me.

So that explains the bespeckled hillside in the distance where brick and stone mounds punctuate the foliage like bamboo shoots after a spring rain. I imagine carloads of people visiting these miniature abodes for the departed, decorating the doorsteps with smoldering incense and whiskey-filled teacups.

My roommate in Taiwan calls me 空中飞人. I use the simplified characters deliberately, even though we are surrounded by traditional script, because she is studying abroad* from Nanjing.

According to my roommate, my 口音 is unplaceable, different from that of any Chinese person she's ever met, different from the handful of white Americans who stand out in the meditation hall and dining room amid neat rows of black-haired and hairless heads.

口音 is such a lovely word, the singular music of each individual maw. It brings to mind the statue of the itinerant tenth-century priest who founded Rokuharamitsu Temple in Kyoto, six buddhas emerging from his open mouth like a procession of pine saplings.

"Accent," on the other hand, is tainted for me, if not by the bitterness of thinly veiled accusation, then by the treacle of compliment-encrusted condescension.†

---

* I suppose her government, which was once my government, wouldn't approve of this characterization. Should I say *studying across the strait*?

† But maybe I'm being too sensitive. Doesn't everyone have an accent?

MY ROOMMATE SAYS I ALMOST sound Taiwanese, but then I'll 卷舌 to reveal a trace of my mainland origins. Can a curl of the tongue let slip so much? She catches me drawling 玩儿 and teases me for it, though I think it fitting for the sportive word to sound like the growl of a dog playing tug-of-war. I counter-tease her for ending *what* sentences with 啥 instead of 什么, sounding to me quite 傻.

But who am I to call her silly? I'm the one who blanks on how to write the second character of her name while returning a book for her. The librarian strains to keep a straight face upon spotting 冰箱 on the ledger. By swapping bamboo for rain, I have turned my roommate into a refrigerator.

I DON'T KNOW HOW TO TRANSLATE 空中飞人. It sounds simultaneously dreamy and sad, like when my aunt says Chinese is my 半母语. My half-mother tongue, taught to me by two moms* who speak four dialects among them. I think my aunt is being generous. These days it's more like my quarter-mother tongue.

There was one other Chinese kid at Little Ducklings day care, a boy who wore a garland of bilingual signs fashioned by his mother. "I want to eat." "I need the potty."† I dreaded the humiliation of wearing my foreignness so baldly. And so it began, the quartering of my native tongue.

I dreaded too my parents' slip of tongues, "tortilla" rhyming with "chinchilla," "geek" sharing the first consonant of "jam." Even more mortifying was my dad's penchant for calling the bathroom a *cisuo*, his native Shanghainese conquering Mandarin in the first syllable. I parroted his habit until a Chinese school teacher witheringly pointed out my error. Even though I never failed to say *CEsuo* thereafter, my dad persists in his Shandarin pronunciation, as if the toilet is in fact a place where porcupines congregate, shedding spiky quills in their wake.

---

* One of them my childhood nanny

† Looking back, I applaud my classmate's ability to read the difference between 我要吃饭 and 我要上厕所. The 文盲 among us immigrant children, illiterate, would not know which to choose for an empty stomach, which for a full bladder.

I WANT TO TRANSLATE 空中飞人 as person-flying-through-space/emptiness. This sounds like a bodhisattva, a person (superhuman?) whose vow to alleviate the suffering of all beings must surely require a lot of this kind of travel. Our first written assignment as chaplain residents was to articulate a "theology of spiritual care." In mine, I waxed poetic about the chaplain as bodhisattva.[*]

The Chinese pop-up dictionary on my computer suggests "trapeze artist" or "frequent flier" for 空中飞人, bursting my bodhisattva bubble in a single mouse-over. I don't have the muscles to be the former. Or the money to be the latter.[†]

The professor who graciously agreed to my unorthodox request to spend a semester at his Buddhist college—despite the fact that I had already completed my master's, despite my not being enrolled in a degree program, despite my mediocre Chinese—invites me to office hours. We speak, oh, sweet respite, in English.

He listens with the gentleness of a sika deer as I fret over my cohort-less status. How to explain *who I am* in the classes I've been sitting in on? Auditor? Visitor? Pseudo-student? I go from classes with first-year undergrads to seminars with advanced graduate students, from the brick-and-tile building that houses the Buddhist studies college to the sleek concrete structures where they are starting four new programs in engaged Buddhism, which makes me . . . ?

The professor says: *You are a wanderer. That is an important vantage point too.*

---

[*] This was before I realized that it's a lot easier to need a bodhisattva than to be one.

[†] Maybe if I was a product manager?

Two juxtaposed GIFs, in a PowerPoint on *WHAT AM I GOING TO DO WITH MY LIFE???*

1) A perfectly coiffed Beyoncé, declaring "I'm not bossy. I'm the boss."
2) A Samoyed in an astronaut suit, floating around inside a spaceship, with the caption "I have no idea what I'm doing."

I am that dog. I wish I could just introduce myself as 空中飞狗.

MY AUNT HELPS ME FIND the words to introduce myself to Chinese-speaking patients at the hospital. This is the aunt who lives in Shanghai, who once thoroughly trounced me at a game of Scrabble when she visited us in Seattle.*

We agree that 宗教师, *religious teacher,* sounds too literal, while 精神支持, *spiritual support[er],* sounds a bit stiff. She muses:

> In Chinese, 精神疏导 or 心理疏导 is quite an occupational term, but 关怀 may sound more humane. Alternatively, you can use 人文关怀 or 心灵关怀, which are both suitable in this case, but may be too extensive in meaning. 神职人员 is awkward for nonbelievers but still embraces a broader sense than 牧师, which is strictly used in the Christian context.

牧师, *shepherd-teacher,* is the translation I encounter most often, but the Lord is not my shepherd and a hospital chaplain's flock is not exclusively Christian.†

I end up explaining not *who I am* but *what I do:* 精神与心理关怀. Or, simply, 关怀. The chaplain's job, distilled to a single word: *care.*

---

* Only teenage hubris can explain my surprise at having lost to a woman who read dictionaries cover to cover during the Cultural Revolution. Did I mention she's a translator and writer?

† Especially not here in the San Francisco Bay Area

PHONE CONVERSATION WITH VISA OFFICER at the Taiwanese consulate in San Francisco [translated from Chinese]:

Officer: 你是什麼?

Me: Excuse me?

Officer: What *are* you?

Me: Umm, 我不是台湾人, I was born in China but I'm an American citizen now . . . so I'm Chinese . . . American . . .

Officer: Do you have a shaved head?

Me: Huh? *[pause]* Oh! No, I'm not a monk, not a nun, I'm just, uh, just an ordinary person. Plain as can be *[nervous chuckle]*. You see, I want to go to the Buddhist monastery to learn more about this thing called . . . well there's lots of ways to say it in Chinese, basically it's like giving spiritual care and support, but actually I'm not a student anymore, but—

Officer *[exasperated]:* So what kind of visa am I supposed to give you?

EVEN BEFORE I BECAME INTERESTED in Buddhism, I would joke that I used to be a dog in a (probably recent) past life. I have a keen sense of smell, a habit of wagging my foot when excited, a toothy happiness when riding in cars with the windows down. My dad must have been ursine rather than canine; he has a recurring dream of standing by a river and catching fish with his bare (sorry) hands (paws?). My mom is too much of an atheist to engage in this kind of speculation.

I know a dedicated Buddhist meditator who thinks that animals are an inferior form of consciousness. Consequently, he refuses to eat them or to keep them as pets. I wonder what he would think about the real reason all those cars are lined up by the graves: not to convene with ancestors, but to honor a much lower form of consciousness.

THAT DREARY DAY, MY MOOD—BURDENED by incessant worry over my nebulous role at the college, darkened by a month of ponderous gray skies—dispatches me off the mountain. The irony of having flown 6,500 miles to a Taiwanese Buddhist monastery only to cut class is not lost on me.

There is no way to go but down. Sullen, I plod on, no spring in my step, no person in sight. I am staring at my worn-out sneakers when suddenly: a sunburst. I lift my head to see a crowd of people.

On the hill nearby, ancestor ghosts resting on the stone slabs of their diminutive front porches, quaffing porcelain thimbles of rice wine and gazing past skinny sentries fast dissolving into whispery piles of ash, see in the distance: a flash of white.

My first thought: a person.

My second thought: short as a child.

My third thought: 白衣觀音!

But no, this is not white-robed Guanyin. This is a crane, not native to these parts. Quickening my steps, I arrive alongside a throng of admirers just as the bird begins to dance.

WITH CHEERFUL ENVY, A MAN in camouflage pronounces me lucky. "I've been waiting all morning, been here four hours already, and as soon as you come the crane starts to dance!"

Other retirees flank the perimeter of the marshy rice paddy. Like my new friend, they are clad in muddy greens and murky browns from head to toe, as if to mask the conspicuousness of their giant telephoto lenses. As if the object of their attention, twenty meters away, might flee upon seeing through their disguised ardor.

The weekday morning slips serenely toward noon.

The crane dances to a symphony of shutters.

The man tells me the story of the bird.

HE FLEW HERE FROM SIBERIA *last winter, came to this rural town a year ago when he still had those tawny baby feathers. No one knows how he ended up here; these birds don't fly all the way to Taiwan. Must've gotten lost.*

Doesn't seem like he'll fly back to Siberia though. Plenty to eat here, a whole rice field to himself with crayfish and lotus roots. He's almost as tall as you or me when his neck's outstretched. Everybody knows about him. He's the reason zoos aren't doing well, you know!

See the way he lifts those wings, hovers a moment, arches that graceful neck, pliés those long legs? He does that when he's happy. That's the moment we're all waiting for.

But you know, it's even more beautiful with a mate. One jumps up as the other lands—they alternate. They bow, they hop, they run, they flap. Now there's a *photo-op for you!*

MY NOT-A-REFRIGERATOR ROOMMATE AND I share many things in common. We were both born in China, both raised by atheist parents. We are not morning people. Our families find it strange, if not downright health-endangering, that we live on a campus where meat is prohibited.

We would both fail the meditation résumé check. Here we are, 在山上, on the mountain, with the perfect conditions for spiritual practice. Daily morning and evening liturgies bookended by hour-long meditation sessions. Week-long retreats throughout the semester. Buddhist monastics leading all of it.

Here we are, sleeping.

Our classmates rise from wood pallets in the predawn, wash faces and brush teeth in the communal bathrooms, sit alert with folded legs in the cavernous gym, chant and bow in the spotless Buddha hall, eat steaming porridge in the cafeteria after their morning ministrations.

Disheveled, my roommate and I stumble into the undarkening dining hall to hastily fill our bowls with the last dregs of congee from a metal pot that the kitchen volunteers are already beginning to wheel away. Abashed, we start skipping breakfast. On the mornings when she has to get up early to study for an exam, I wake to birdsong and the crunch of instant noodles eaten straight from the package.

WHEN I WAS STILL IN California preparing to go to Taiwan, my roommate was meditating for the first time. The weeklong silent retreat was mandatory for all incoming students of the Buddhist college. She soldiered through spartan conditions only to emerge haggard from days of inexplicable vomiting.

My introduction to meditation, when I was around her age,* came more gently. After three months of regular vipassana and Zen practice, I embarked on my first silent meditation retreat, five days and four nights in Northern California. We slept two to a room on comfy mattresses in our woodsy chambers, pondered a vast menagerie of tea in the kitchen during break times, sipped our individual selections while trying not to think about whether the lemon echinacea or hibiscus rose or vanilla rooibos would have been a better choice. Oh, yes—and we meditated too.

---

* She calls me 姐姐, as to be expected given our eight-year age gap. I can't bring myself to call her 妹妹 though. Too infantilizing, and besides, I'm the one who can't even write her name correctly.

I DOUBT I WOULD HAVE been at that retreat in Northern California if I didn't believe, to a certain degree, that meditation would make me a better Buddhist— or a better person, because I wasn't yet calling myself a Buddhist then.

Yes, just notice what arises. Yes, non-attachment to the outcome. And yet. I can't resist the siren call of better, that relentless tread toward self-improvement. A familiar road: It is 1999, I am thirteen, my hamster died a week ago, I write in my journal, "lose weight, 1 lb., I am 93 right now."

And so it begins. There has to be a better tea out there, a better me out there. Surely meditating is better than starving myself?

MEDITATION MISHAPS:

1) Junior year of college, I attend the daily meditation sessions of the on-campus Buddhist student group. The only other regular has been meditating since the age of thirteen.* We sit in a cramped closet of a room as morning sun ekes in through vinyl blinds that conceal the tiniest of windows. I am feeling proud not to have budged from my lotus position for the past thirty minutes, screaming pain in hip be damned. My long-legged, flexible-hipped companion marks the end of the session: *ding!* He stands up lithely, cushion and bell in hand. I hasten to follow, realize too late that my foot is asleep, fall and twist my ankle.

2) In grad school, I mention to a fellow student in the Buddhist chaplaincy program that I don't have a meditation practice—that, to be honest, I don't particularly like meditating. Alarm flits across her face, as if I am a dentist who has just confessed to never flossing, a pulmonologist caught smoking. "Don't worry; that will change," she blurts out. I'm not sure which of us she's trying to reassure.

3) Now, when I could be meditating, I write. Or sleep.

---

* He does not tell me he is the club's president until three months after we start dating.

SOMEWHERE ALONG THE WAY, I had become convinced that to be a good Buddhist is to be a good meditator. It does not occur to me to interrogate what "good" might mean in this equation.

Not until the Buddhist boyfriend and I move to Southeast Asia will I realize that this equivalence renders the world full of bad Buddhists. Like the Cambodians who converge by the brothy Tonle Sap on full- and half- and new-moon days, lotus buds and incense sticks in hand, awaiting their turn to make offerings at the riverfront shrine. Like our neighbor in Phnom Penh, whom we call Lok Yeay (grandmother), who nonchalantly gives us local fruit and begrudgingly cares for stray cats and offhandedly mentions that we shouldn't assume she'll still be alive after our weeklong trip to Laos.* Regular temple-goers whose actions bespeak generosity and non-attachment and impermanence—but can they really represent Buddhism without its sine qua non, that cross-legged practice par excellence so glowingly embodied by svelte yoginis on glossy magazine covers?

The summer after my first year of grad school, I attend a ten-day workshop on Guanyin, the goddess of mercy who first arrived in China from India in the guise of the male bodhisattva Avalokitesvara. We are based, aptly enough, near Putuoshan,† a pilgrimage site to which Guanyin devotees flock. After the workshop, with a day to spare before catching the train to Shanghai, I take the earliest morning ferry over. Meandering along the island's roads through forests and beaches, I chance upon a young Chinese couple on vacation. They tell me they aren't Buddhist, though one of them used to go to temple with her grandmother to 拜拜, praying for good grades with three perfunctory nods of the head, cough-inducing joss sticks sandwiched between her palms. The couple apologizes for the superstitions of this older generation. Is it true that in America, even ordinary run-of-the-mill people who aren't monks or nuns meditate? Now isn't that a truer form of Buddhism?

Somewhere along the way, I had become convinced that to be a good Buddhist is to be a white meditator.

---

* Despite our protestations that she is the spitting image of vigor. You never know, she shrugs, and we have to concede that she's right. *We* might not come back alive from Laos.

† One of the four sacred mountains of Chinese Buddhism, and the only one that is also an island

ANOTHER MISHAP? (BAY AREA, POST-COLLEGE, pre–grad school.)

At the final monthly meeting of an introduction to Buddhist chaplaincy training program, we are invited to take our teachers' places. Each of us ascends the stage to field questions from the other nineteen students and (nerve-rackingly) our three instructors.

The stage is a modest one. What at a temple might be dais on wood is, at this meditation center, zafu on carpet. Come my turn, something isn't right. I can't bring myself to sit on the plump black cushion.

Instead, I'm drawn to the low coffee table graced by a small Buddha statue, humble compared to altars I've seen elsewhere.* In front of the lone Buddha statue, I bow three times. Head dipped, hands in prayer, hands to forehead, hands to heart, a deep bend in the knees, knees on carpet, palms and forehead follow, the whole sequence in reverse to rise—all of this thrice repeated.

Bemused, our teachers (all white, all meditators) ask: Why did you bow?

I must have babbled an answer, face aflame. But truth be told, I don't know. I didn't grow up bowing, so why would I do it now?

Why do I envy the people—so visible in Asia, so invisible here—for whom these acts of devotion are inscribed in body memory, performed without self-consciousness, effortless? Effortless the way my elementary school class mates fixed themselves bowls of cereal. Classmates pale as cold milk, milk my grandma would have insisted I heat up had she been with us in that semirural town in Pennsylvania, but 奶奶 was in Shanghai then and wouldn't come to America for another fifteen years, arriving shortly after the Buddhist boyfriend informs me that pouring the milk before dumping on the Cheerios is not the standard order of operations for this procedure.†

---

* In Cambodia: stone Tathagatas standing and seated, encircled by lotuses and psychedelic halos radiating rainbow beams of neon light. In San Francisco: Shakyamuni flanked by Guanyin and Kshitigarbha, surrounded by orchids and trays piled high with polished orbs of fruit.

† So *that's* why those tiny flotation devices would leap out of the bowl like the Monkey King on a mission, instead of diving dutifully to the bottom of the milky lake like a bodhisattva rescuing the drowning . . .

Why does it feel comforting to bow, a motion as unpracticed for me as pouring cereal first, milk after? Before the puzzled eyes of my classmates and teachers, I feel like a chinawoman in a canary, although I don't think that's how the expression goes.

"HAVE YOU EVER THOUGHT ABOUT the 因緣, all the karmic causes and conditions, that made it possible for you to be here with us in this moment?" my favorite professor at the Buddhist college asks us one day in her Topics in Holistic Education class.

Here I am, a Chinese American former chaplain among Taiwanese students of wide-ranging ages and professions, some of whom were not even raised Buddhist. . . . Wait. How *did* we end up here?

Silence settles thickly upon the room as the twenty of us think back to the choices and coincidences, loves and sorrows, lives and deaths, vows and caprices, that have coalesced into this very now.

"IF YOU CUT SOMEONE OFF and then can't find a parking space, that's not karma, that's poetic justice!"

So exclaims one of the young adults I interviewed for my master's thesis on Asian American Buddhists. She can't help but feel exasperated by the way "karma" is bandied about in popular culture. Maybe this has something to do with her Vietnamese Buddhist parents, even if she can't remember the last time they went to temple together, not even for Tết.

Another one of my interviewees can't help but *gassho* to the Buddha statue at the cannabis club. His favorite Buddhist concept is *ichi-go ichi-e,* which he illustrates using the example at hand. "It's like this interview," he explains. "Like we're meeting for the first time, and actually I thought you were a man—sorry, it's just that with your name it's hard to tell—but anyway, even if we did this again, it could never be the same. First of all, I would know you're not a dude, but *even* if we both got amnesia and forgot about our entire conversation today, it's like we've been *changed* from this encounter, and we can't unchange that, right?"

And what about the events we wish we *could* change? The tragedies of history. How can we understand the workings of karma on a collective level when faced with, say, all the deaths during the Khmer Rouge period?* When I pose this question to Thanissaro Bhikkhu, who has just given a talk on karma at my alma mater, the American Buddhist monk cites the Acintita Sutta. The results of karma are unconjecturable, bringing vexation to those who try to figure out its precise workings. In other words: Let it be. The exact mechanisms of karma are not for you to know. Such an inquiry can only lead to madness.

---

* A memory: En route to Tibet during a gap year between high school and college, I get lost on the dusty streets of Kathmandu. A zealous missionary strikes up a conversation, then won't stop following me. He insists on praying for my hell-bound soul. A laying on of hands: I freeze, thinking how effortless it would be for this former rugby player's meaty fingers to scarve around my neck and piously extinguish my heathen breath. Before he lets me go, the missionary says, *You see? You Asiatics get what you deserve, like that earthquake and tsunami.* He means the recent catastrophe in Indonesia that killed nearly 300,000 people.

IN ADDITION TO POSING BROW-KNITTING questions, my favorite professor in Taiwan likes to make art and give it away. At the end of the semester, knowing I won't be returning for the next one, she presses a card deck–sized block of balsa wood into my palm. She's seared four characters into the burnished blond surface: 一期一會.

I can read the characters, but I don't recognize the expression. "It's Japanese," she prompts. "Do you know it?"

I'm about to say no when the ghost of high school Japanese class past suggests I try reading 一 as *ichi*. A phrase with two *ichi*s . . . Yes! Someone once explained it to me. A cannabis club–going Buddha-respecting fourth-generation Japanese American, to be precise, but that's probably more than she needs to know.

THE BUDDHIST BOYFRIEND'S SISTER-IN-LAW'S FATHER is prone to aphorisms. At Thanksgiving dinner, apropos of nothing, he proclaims, "Best laid plans go awry!"

It's true. I did not intend to pursue an education in Buddhist chaplaincy. I had no plans to watch a peerless Russian crane dance in Taiwan.

On the mountain, they spoke of 緣分, the karmic affinities whose knotted roots we cannot disentangle.

> *White crane white crane brilliant white, of what do you dream at night?*
> *Do you dream of kith and kin, or does your memory of them wear thin?*
> *Did you intend to sojourn here, to become a stranger odd and dear?*

TWO-HOUR POWERPOINT PRESENTATION FOR TOPICS in Holistic Education, delivered in Mandarin by yours truly:*

1) Title Slide

   • Clinical Pastoral Education (CPE) & Chaplaincy in America: Reflections from a Buddhist CPE Student's Perspective

   • Disclaimers: I speak from limited experience. Please forgive my poor Chinese.

2) Outline

   • What is chaplaincy?

     ▪ Challenges of translation

     ▪ A brief history

     ▪ The role of Buddhists

   • How are chaplains trained?

     ▪ Professional organizations

     ▪ Clinical Pastoral Education 臨床牧關(?)教育課程

     ▪ My experiences as a yearlong resident

3) Translation Issues

   • Chaplaincy is not well understood, even in the US

     ▪ Upon introducing myself to one patient, he jumped up and shouted, "I'm not dying yet!" Another man hollered: "I'm not Christian! Get out!" Another regarded me with suspicion: "I thought you'd be an old fart ..." (not yet; give me a few years).

   • For most of American history, chaplains have indeed been predominantly Christian (and male, and white). Now, the field of chaplaincy is diversifying.

   • I've struggled to translate "chaplain" and "chaplaincy" into Chinese

     ▪ 宗教師 and 牧師: associated with Christianity, connotation is more specifically religious than broadly spiritual

---

* "If you want me to give you a two-hour presentation, I am ready today. If you want only a five-minute speech, it will take me two weeks to prepare." If only Twain's maxim were true. I spent two months on this two-hour presentation.

- 神職人員: a translation of "religious professional" used by the hospital, but don't you think it sounds a bit awkward?
- 精神護理／精神支持, 精神與心理關懷: when I met Chinese-speaking patients at the hospital, I usually opted for this description. Many assumed I was a volunteer or a church employee, and were surprised to learn I was technically employed by the hospital.
- Since coming to Taiwan, I've heard other translations: 心理／精神疏導, 人文關懷, 心靈關懷, 靈性照顧

- I will use the words "chaplain" and "chaplaincy" in English for this presentation
  - Etymology/origin of the word "chaplain"
    - *cappella,* "little cloak" in medieval Latin

4) St. Martin of Tours (or, Why a Cloak?)

- This fourth-century Christian saint was the bishop of Tours. His shrine in France became a famous stopping point for pilgrims.
- Pre-sainthood, as a soldier in the Roman army stationed in Gaul (modern-day France), Martin met a beggar clad only in rags in the depth of winter. Using his military sword to cut his cloak in two, Martin gave one half to the beggar.
- He dreamed of Jesus wearing half a cloak. Upon waking, Martin's cloak had become whole.
- The cloak became a relic. The priest who cared for the cloak in its reliquary was called a *cappellanu.*
- Eventually, priests who served the military were called *cappellani.* The French translation is *chapelains,* from which the English word "chaplain" is derived.
- Some chaplains use this metaphor to show how we comfort those we serve. We give others a part of—but not our *entire*—cloak, because it's no use freezing to death ourselves!

5) Chaplains in the US Military

- The Old Testament refers to priests accompanying troops into battle

- 1775, George Washington: "The Continental Congress having been pleased to order, and direct, that there shall be one Chaplain to two Regiments . . ."

- Currently more than 3,000 chaplains serve in the armed forces

6) Buddhist Chaplains in the Military

- In 1990 the American military finally made plans for the inclusion of Buddhist chaplains

- WWII Nisei (second-generation Japanese Americans)

  - A 1944 service for 50 soldiers at Fort Snelling is believed to be the first Buddhist service ever delivered in an army installation in the United States

  - A majority of Nisei troops were Buddhist

  - However, Nisei units such as the 442nd were only allowed to have Christian chaplains. Assistant Secretary of Defense John J. McCloy feared that negative American perceptions of Buddhists would compromise the reputation of the unit.

7) Chaplains in the US Government

- House of Representatives

  - First House Chaplain: Rev. William Linn, selected in 1789

  - Current (60th) House Chaplain: Patrick Conroy, selected in 2011

- Senate

  - First Senate Chaplain: Samuel Provoost, selected in 1789

  - Current (62nd) Senate Chaplain: Barry Black, the first African American and first Seventh Day Adventist to hold the post, selected in 2003

- A Buddhist has never held either post

24) Closing Observations on Chaplaincy in America

- Christian-dominated field, God-focused/theistic language and assumptions

- US-centric/Western-oriented—lack of global perspectives

- Here in Taiwan, you would expect Buddhist chaplains to be monastics rather than laypeople; in America, you're more likely to see the opposite

- Bible verses abound; references to Buddhist texts . . . not so much

- Serving diverse populations while staying rooted in our Buddhist traditions is an ongoing challenge

25) P.S.

- Chaplaincy is a profession, not just something volunteers do

- In the US, Buddhists are ~1% of the population. Two-thirds of American Buddhists are of Asian heritage, but I have met only a handful of Asian American Buddhist chaplains.

Any questions?

. . .

. . .

. . .

Oh, dear. That might have been information overload. Everybody is looking downright bulldozed. Which is exactly how I felt for most of my CPE year.

AT THE MUSIC PARTY WHERE her coworker interrogates me into the refrigerator, my mom sings a song I have never heard before.

不要问我从哪里来	Do not ask me where I come from
我的故乡在远方	My hometown is far away
为什么流浪	Why do I wander?
流浪远方	Wander afar
流浪	Wandering
为了天空飞翔的小鸟	For the birds that soar in the sky
为了山间轻流的小溪	For the brooks that flow in the hills
为了宽阔的草原	For the vast grasslands
流浪远方	Wandering afar
流浪	Wandering
还有还有	And too, and too,
为了梦中的橄榄树	For my dreamed olive tree
橄榄树*	Olive tree

Hear this plaintive melody that quiets even the young children gathered round. Who is that with tears streaming down her cheeks?

　　(The singer's only daughter—what was it she said her job was? Couldn't make heads or tails of it . . .)

---

* Song lyrics by 三毛

BIG BIRD IS GRIEVING THE DEATH of Mr. Hooper, who ran the neighborhood store.

Yellow feathers aquiver, Big Bird cries, "Well, I don't understand! . . . Why does it have to be this way?"

His friends watch on in pained silence. Finally, Gordon responds, "It has to be this way . . . because."

Big Bird asks, "Just because?"

Gordon replies, "Just because."

Big Bird says, "Oh."

And then all of his friends engulf him in a giant hug.

—*An exemplary chaplaincy moment, brought to you by* Sesame Street

DEVOTION:

    The white crane dances for an invisible beloved.

    The camouflaged people come to watch.

    I want, inexplicably, to cry.

    Those feathery arms could wrap me whole.

    I would worship at this outdoor church every day.

I DON'T MANAGE TO MAKE the long walk to that open-air church every day, not even every week. But before I leave Taiwan, I make sure to visit once more. It's a rainy day. Gray clouds curtain the low hills. The devotees balance umbrellas and cameras.

There are a couple other birds knee-deep in the flooded field, looking squat and drab compared to the area's (island's? country's?) most famous avian resident. I wonder if they ever get jealous. Birdwatchers used to come to this area to admire their ilk, but *Leucogeranus leucogeranus* has stolen the show.

An elderly Taiwanese man walks the tightrope of concrete that serves as the only mud-free path through his fields. He wears black galoshes and denim jeans, a blue jacket and a tangerine-colored baseball cap. He has the morning paper in one hand; I half-expect a mug of coffee in the other.

The figure in white takes mincing steps toward the crown of tangerine. They regard each other for a minute, just like when they first met, before the news spread, before the worshippers came in droves.

The Siberian émigré and the Taiwanese farmer. Old friends grown accustomed to the amicable silence of each other's company.

They stroll past each other on the narrow path, continuing in opposite directions, carrying on with their days.

I WONDER IF THE CRANE feels safe or constrained, watched so. If he is happily monastic or bracingly lonely. What language he speaks, what colors he dreams in. If he misses Siberia.

I wonder if the crane will fly away someday. How many of us will cry then. If we will shed our tears in private or let them escape in the presence of kindred others who can no longer imagine this place without him.

I want to ask the crane: *What were you before you were born? What will you be after you die?*

FAREWELL POST FROM THE PROFESSOR who asked how we all ended up here on the mountain:

一期一會
明天辰星就要出發到柬埔寨了
知道她愛貓
在離開前帶她去看最可愛的柚子
那被辰星笑稱為青少年的調皮傢伙
趕在我們出店前回來撒嬌

這個學期辰星和我們一起生活一起學習
從大學國文到生命教育研究
也參與到金山醫院的社區安寧與長照關懷
這位可愛的上海出生美國長大的姑娘
帶著靈性關懷師的學習與工作背景
給大家帶來許多的支持與陪伴

祝福到柬埔寨之後
完成那本書，持續支持需要照顧的人

Ichi-go ichi-e
Tomorrow Chenxing will be off to Cambodia
Knowing she loves cats
I took her to see the most adorable Pomelo
that tabby whom Chenxing laughingly called a rascally teenager
rushed back to the café right before we left, pouting for another
     scratch behind the ears

This semester Chenxing lived and learned with us

from College-Level Chinese Literature to Topics in Holistic
　　Education

to Jinshan Hospital's community program for hospice and
　　long-term care

This lovely young woman, born in Shanghai and raised in America

with her chaplaincy education and training

supported and accompanied us all

Blessings for her time in Cambodia

finish that book, keep supporting those who need care

PART II: 杯弓蛇影

shadow/snake

A LETTER TO THE YOUNG WOMAN who was once my college roommate:

Dearest,

You said, fall is the most honest season. It does not pretend that life blooms forever.

People could be excused for thinking only of summer upon first meeting you, your petite frame alight with that unruly crest of golden curls.

We could be excused for thinking your life would bloom forever, even though you knew, from an impossibly early age, that it would be more evanescent than most.

Fall, your favorite season. The season of cold and sun, rain and warmth, clear mornings and color-soaked trees. Everywhere reminders of impermanence.

Please excuse me, 原谅我, ขอประทานโทษ, 許してください, សូមអញ្ជាស្រ័យ, *in all the languages I know or half-know or barely know, please forgive me, poor student of the most basic of Buddhist tenets:* All phenomena arise and pass away.

Still, that final fall came so swiftly. I had dared to hope for a dozen more. On sunny days, two dozen. And in my hope I grew forgetful.

FIVE MONTHS AFTER LEAVING TAIWAN, I receive an email from the wood-carving professor:

雖然很掙扎
但想想還是跟妳說
柚子在我們上回去吃飯之後沒多久
因為在外頭玩
不小心吃到老鼠藥
已經往生了
主人很傷心, 覺得牠在人間時間太短了
但我相信柚子能得這麼多人愛
一定會去到美好的地方重生

Though torn
I thought I must tell you
Not long after we ate together at the café, Pomelo
while playing outside
accidentally ingested rat poison
and has already passed on to the next life
The owner was devastated, lamenting that he was among us for too
    brief a time
But I trust Pomelo, loved by so many
will be reborn to a glorious place

THE BUDDHIST CHAPLAINCY STUDENTS AT my grad school are required to take one class from a Jodo Shinshu minister who is age-dappled but still dapper. There is only one assignment for the entire semester: write an essay about your spiritual journey and read it out loud to your classmates. We ask for more direction: how long, what format, where to begin. He chuckles and offers only one suggestion: "The more suffering the better."

The same reverend also says: "Chaplaincy is one of those things where it's hard when you're in it, but then you look back and find the lessons and gifts."

He pauses.

"But really, all of life is like this."

ONE YEAR AFTER TAKING THE reverend's class, I trade my student ID for a hospital badge. I am one of five chaplaincy residents in this year's CPE program. As with the staff chaplains, we are each assigned to different units across the three Bay Area hospital campuses. I'm tasked with covering the oncology and medical/renal floors at The Tower.* The building's nickname is justified only by its stubbier cousins, the psychiatric hospital and the hospital Where All the Babies Are Born.

As the only member of the spiritual care team who speaks Mandarin, I sometimes get referred to other units. A fellow resident asks me to visit a woman on rehab, per the request of the patient's daughter, who has to work during the day. Daughter is worried about Mom, who is recovering from surgery after the blindsiding cancer diagnosis. Mom's ability to communicate in English is limited. Can a Chinese-speaking chaplain check in?

At the end of a full day of visits, I follow up on the referral. For a disorienting moment after the elevator doors open, I fear I've developed face blindness. The upper floors of The Tower all have the same layout, so it looks like I haven't gone anywhere—yet I can't recognize a single staff member. Then I spot an occupational therapist helping a stroke survivor take tentative steps down the hall. I notice how much calmer it is than medical/renal, a unit so hectic the nurses seek respite by rotating to the ER. Like oncology, there's an atmosphere of lingering here on rehab, different from the floor below where patients stay a strict three days before going home with mended hearts.

Mrs. J's door is open. She is working with an occupational therapist who speaks Mandarin. I offer to come back another time, but the OT is finishing up. She says she'll leave Mrs. J to meet with—here she squints at my badge—the chaplain here. She says all of this in Chinese except for the word "chaplain."

I explain my role in the best colloquial Mandarin I can muster. Mrs. J cuts off my meandering introduction: "I don't want to talk about religion!"

I stammer that we don't, um, need to talk about religion, 随便聊聊天也可以.

So then we do just that. We shoot the breeze, that afternoon and many thereafter, until Mrs. J is discharged from the hospital.

---

* An optimistic moniker, considering how the elevator buttons barely eke into double digits

DEVOTIONS:

My first month on the oncology unit, it seemed the hospital was full of pairs. One mate wounded and the other tending. One partner sleeping and the other holding—her hand, his breath, a swab, their child, the tray.

No one told me this work would be full of love stories.

Long after I've forgotten the couple's names and faces, long after her medical chart details have melted into digital soup, the memory of their love lingers, boiled down to a single word spoken with carefree habit: *Angelpie*.

It's almost embarrassing, in this age of swipe-shopping for romance, to witness such intimacy. Another long-married couple reflects on the disposability of relationships these days. With furtive smiles and gleaming eyes they recall cross-country trips by motorbike, before two became five. Thick as thieves, they await the inevitable, that invisible sixth who will come to steal their husband/father away. (Come to steal all of us away, someday.) They invite me in. Pull up a chair, chaplain, gather round. The tribe is thinning. Join the vigil. Now is for story time and celebration. The air is carbonated with laughter, clear of pity.

Another day, a different room. *We are the best of friends,* the high school sweethearts tell me. They want only to return to their RV and their cat, humble trappings of an adoration that has only deepened over the decades.

There is the husband I never see leave his wife's side. He assures me that she, twenty years his elder, is the smarter, better-looking one, bald head and chemo brain notwithstanding. They come to the oncology unit more often (and for far longer) than they'd like. Each time, he's confident that any day now they'll be going home. Home, where her pillows are plumped, his workstation strategically situated to refluff them at a moment's notice.

I meet an electrician who never married. She's always been good with her hands, got used to being the only woman in the room. Long-time union member, civil rights activist, lover of birds. This amazon with wool scarf for head feathers tells me: *My parakeet got ovarian cancer the same time I did. We've gone through treatment together.* I feel suddenly 心酸, a squeeze of lime inside my chest. *Is she ok,* I ask, and the electrician begins to cry. *Yes, for now. We're ok for now.*

A SMALL SAMPLE OF THE unexpected things you learn as a chaplain:

Parakeets can get ovarian cancer.

You best be careful when alligator hunting lest a sloppy bullet ruin the leather you're after.

Even unflappable nurses can be fazed, as when the patient who doesn't want to be discharged is forcibly removed—but not before throwing a fit of rage that leaves his hospital room and the security guards strewn with cremains.

THE ALLIGATOR VISIT BEGINS ON a gruff note. Curt would be an apt name for this patient, who is more than ready to be done being a patient. He interrupts my introduction with a growl.

"I don't need anything. I just need an apartment."

His has burned down, which is why he's here, for smoke inhalation. I remember him from last week's morning rounds with the interdisciplinary team.

"You look a lot better than when you first came in," I note.

Curt grunts noncommittally. His gaze is glued to the TV, where a trio of men float peacefully downriver.

I figure this conversation is going nowhere and am about to excuse myself when Curt interjects.

"Would you want to do that?" I realize he's been tracking me out of the corner of his eye.

"Sure, it looks nice, reminds me of when I used to visit my mom in Florida."

He chuckles. "Naw, you don't want to do that."

"What do you mean?"

"You know what they're doing? No?"

I'm at a loss.

"Shootin' alligators!"

Onscreen, one of the gators is now thrashing around, bloodying the muddy waters.

"You gotta watch where you put that bullet! Don't wanna mess up the hide."

Well I'll be . . . that would never have occurred to me. We chat a bit longer. I resist the temptation to bid farewell with a pun, though I can almost hear the echo of "after a while, crocodile" as I leave.

SO. YOU NEVER KNOW WHERE shooting the breeze might lead, to alligator hunting, to parakeet cancer, to the very topic the patient vowed not to broach. "I don't want to talk about religion!" But eventually Mrs. J is the one to bring up her philosophy of living and her equanimity around dying.

"It's my daughter I'm worried about," she confesses. "Working full time, visiting me every day, caring for the kids—those little ones are the reason I moved here from Taiwan, you know—and now on top of all that tending to an injured husband." Though we've never met, I feel the presence of this daughter— capable, fierce, protective—in every visit.

Mrs. J insists I address her as J 媽媽, Mama J. I could call her J 老師—after all, she was a schoolteacher for decades in her Taiwanese hometown—but she prefers the kinship term. Over the weeks, I watch her grandchildren's colorful artwork gain purchase over the sterile walls of her Bay Area hospital room.

When patients get discharged from the hospital, I offer blessings, thinking of my 奶奶. My father's mother, my nainai, would say to me before every trip, 一路順風. A benediction that cloaked me in warm winds, gentle breezes she entrusted to bring her granddaughter back safe and sound. 一路順風 a magic spell, my protective amulet.

When patients get discharged from the hospital, I wish them *god bless* or *take care* or *be well*, but when the language is English I do not say "Hope to see you again," because wouldn't that mean seeing them back in the hospital? But in Chinese it's impossible not to say 再见, a farewell so ubiquitous I forget its literal meaning: [let's] again meet. The day she leaves the hospital, I say *zaijian* to Mama J and her daughter, who is indeed capable, fierce, and protective, who has gotten off work early and is efficiently emptying the room, eager to bring Mom home at last.

Tasked with impromptu prayer
at the foot of M's hospital deathbed,
I borrow her family's belief in God,
scrounge courage in sips
of scrubbed air.

Amid garbled generalities,
a specificity
tumbles from
my trembling tongue
at the sight of
her painted toenails:
This is a woman with *style.*

Her family smiles.

Holy and human witnesses
to colorful keratin and
the absence of breath.

Wistfully, her sister says to the stillness:
Girl, *I am going*
to miss
seeing you
in those stilettos.

GRAN'MA, YOU HELD US TOGETHER . . .

Auntie, you gave me the courage . . .

Her husband touches the painted toenails and whispers to his beloved,

   Honey, I'll see you again . . .

Dearest one,

Just after your diagnosis, I send you an email with the subject line "Beauty." I attach a photo of fuchsia flowers outside the gate of the National Museum, just down the street from us in Phnom Penh.

There are thirty-three emails in that thread, seven from you. A pet peeve we share: people who begin emails with salutationless thuds, not even bothering with a dear/hi/hey/yo/whassup. We will never write to each other with just the other's name followed by a comma. If the name leads, then it must always be followed by love. The cure for my middle-namelessness: all those letters from you that begin Chenxing love. *I am thinking of this when I read the first lines of the first of those seven emails: "Dearest of dearest you, I love you. So much. Beyond words, actually."*

You write about your plans to fly from Portland to the transplant center in Minnesota as early as tomorrow morning. "It is a wild time. There is sadness, fear, grief, and also this inescapable love and gratitude that is carrying me."

On chemo day two, you write, "I've been trying to focus on the warmth, the humor, the gratitude of what it means to be here . . . and there is so much of that every day—from kind visitors, to the nurse in the hallway who offered to roll up my pant cuffs, stating, Just because you're here doesn't mean you don't get to be sexy."

IF YOU THINK CHAPLAINS SHOULD be strait-laced and staid, one of our staff chaplains will have you thinking again. She wears high heels with confidence, cuts a figure impossibly tall as she strides purposefully down the hospital halls. The patients don't always remember our names, but I always know when they're referring to her. They wanna know when they'll see the really well-dressed lady chaplain again.

Another one of our staff chaplains has been working here so long he's known as the mayor of the hospital. On the very first day of our residency program, the mayor gives us a guided tour of The Tower. He takes us to the viewing room in the basement. Ashen-faced, we take notes. Don't worry, he tells us jollily—it'll become second nature in no time. Once, on a particularly busy day, he found himself in this very room, weighing down the eyes of the deceased with one hand while holding a peanut butter and jelly sandwich in the other. The PB&J meant no irreverence. It was, in fact, an act of consideration. He didn't want to delay the viewing, and it would hardly do the family any good for their chaplain to pass out from hunger on them.

The mayor is showing us what we residents will all, in our early enthusiasm, neglect: Chaplains must be unwavering in their self-care. Naive and eager at first, we offer ourselves so fully—too fully. We freeze from offering our whole cloaks. We faint from forgetting to eat. In the thrall of others' stories, we fail to attend to our own.

THE VIEWING ROOM CAN FIT a gurney. At the gurney's head is a small table. On the table perches a digital clock, a box of Kleenex, and a black landline phone. Portable chairs kiss the gurney's sides.

It is our job:

To arrange for the body to be prepared (by environmental services,* or am I misremembering?) and wheeled to the room (by transportation services).

To check that the body looks presentable (wear gloves, make gentle adjustments as needed).

To make sure the white sheets are tucked (try to conceal the body bag that has been unzipped and peeled back for this occasion).

To ensure that the single window in the room is curtained off from the adjacent room (where there are supplies such as gloves and hospital gowns— and an extra freezer in case the morgue gets full, or am I misremembering?).

To guide the family down the special elevator and explain what they can expect (your loved one will be cold to the touch, his eyes are slightly open, her jaw is agape).

To unlock the heavy door with our ID badges and then, in whatever way is most appropriate, to host the viewing (no two are ever the same).

---

* *Environmental services (EVS):* hospital-speak for the hardworking employees who empty the wastebaskets and mop the floors and wipe the cremains from the walls. They must clean every room on their units, a quota of visits that exacts a physical and emotional toll, especially when they are also worried about their mother in Honduras, their son not doing well in school, their recently laid-off husband. For months I thought this department had the strangest name, until I realized how its people—reduced in title to function, abstraction, acronym—are an indispensable and invisible part of the hospital ecosystem, as necessary and taken for granted as air.

WHEN THE MAYOR WALKS THROUGH the hospital, he leaves behind a trail of brightened faces. He says "Hello, how are you?" and waits for the answer. He is handsome in tailored suits. A spare, freshly pressed, hangs inside the door to his office at all times.

Given his excellent sartorial sense, it's not surprising that the mayor is the mastermind behind the hospital's clothing closet, a curated collection of donated items organized by size and color. The mayor's initiative has spared those patients with nary a shirt to their name the indignity of leaving the hospital in those shapeless gowns that invariably make the wearer look like a frog with a bad case of chickenpox.

Dear one,

You would not be caught dead in such a gown. (Literally.*) The CaringBridge updates from your hospital room could double as a fashion blog.

Here is a photo of you with your head shaved, right hand tucked inside a lobster-claw oven mitt, claw-mitt pinching a stick that has a fake mustache glued to its end—black handlebars quivering above your white hospital mask. (I'm pretty sure Halloween is still a couple months away? But no matter!)

In another photo, you are wearing a black-and-white bateau shirt with a jaunty red felt hat, opening a package containing—I agree with you, there is nothing better than—patterned fuzzy socks.

In another, you're in horse pose, aquamarine tank top, black yoga pants, Elsa-from-Frozen headscarf.

Then lying in the hospital bed in a purple top and lavender knit cap, next to you a homemade cake smothered in chocolate-vanilla-swirl icing, a riot of balloons all around. (Your birthday won't be for another six months, but no matter.)

Another day it's a pink shirt, pink hat, striped socks (magenta and white on the right foot, blue and white on the left foot).

The SLOFFEE T-shirt with an image of your favorite slow-moving arboreal mammal in a cup of joe.

You were radiant in blue hospital scrubs (the fiancé handsome in red ones) on your pulled-together-in-a-flash wedding day. (How lucky to have woken up in Phnom Penh and seen the message just in time to join the video-ceremony—had I slept another hour I would've missed it.)

And my favorite: the custom printed hot pink shirt that reads, in rounded capital letters, OFFICIALLY—followed by your newly minted married name.

---

* *I don't think you would find this truth flippant or morbid of me. You who from a precocious age insisted that it's better just to say* died *than* passed *or* left *or* gone to a better place *or any of the countless other euphemisms people use. You who shared my enthusiasm for* Someone I Love Died, *a children's book gifted to me in Cape Town by a nonprofit specializing in bereavement for South African youth. You who once wrote to me about "the stack I'm bringing with me to Bend: an odd mixture of poetry, children's books, and a sizable chunk of books on death, intermixed of course with plenty of Kai Skye—these things we accumulate over time."*

SOME OF THE RESIDENTS CAN'T wait to do their first viewing. I am dreading it. Dreading it and all the other firsts we have been diligently taking notes to prepare ourselves for. First code gray. First code blue. First on-call shift. First patient death. First fetal demise (a special category of patient death).

We are just learning the ropes. How is it that as soon as these two weeks of orientation are over, we will be expected to *know* the ropes? People will look at our CHAPLAIN badges and locate power, authority. I can barely locate the nearest bathroom. It took me half an hour to find my car on the first day because I was looking in the wrong parking lot. People are going to see me as a representative of God? (I pity the god who is this directionally challenged.) Can they not see the wild fear and utter unpreparedness in my eyes?

Two weeks of orientation draws to a close. We've gotten our vaccines, one of which I had a violent allergic reaction to. I've gone through the rigmarole of yet another chest X-ray—the smallpox vaccine scar beneath my left bicep, a marker of my birth in China, is also a reminder that TB skin tests will always trigger a false positive for me.

We've done the fetal demise didactic,* taught by the tough, funny, intimidating trickster of a chaplain whom I think of as the mayor of the other hospital campus, the campus Where All the Babies Are Born—and a very few stillborn. Her PowerPoint is filled with images of malformed fetuses. She'd rather us be shocked now than in front of the families. Besides, she chortles, beauty is in the eye of the beholder. One woman cradled her cyclops baby's lifeless body and crooned over how perfect he was, *don't you think so too, chaplain?* Our trickster, not prone to lying and hardly demure, must have found some way to demur.

---

* *Didactic:* a rather stiff name for the various presentations and workshops that supplement our patient visits. Other activities that distinguish residents from staff chaplains include our weekly one-on-one supervision meetings and process group, a.k.a. IPR (CPE-speak for "interpersonal relations group").

DEMURE COULD BE MY MIDDLE name. People used to call me "Mousey" in high school. What have I gotten myself into?

At the end of orientation, each of the new residents is paired with a staff chaplain. I take a deep breath. Shadowing. Shadowing I can do. As I follow the suited figure through the hospital, my nervousness eases. Our path to the unit is a tunnel of warm greetings.

On the first visit, the mayor takes the lead, introducing himself to the patient and explaining that "his colleague"—I realize with a jolt that he's referring to me—will watch, is that ok? Before the second visit, he says, let's do this one jointly, I'll introduce myself, you introduce yourself. I blanch—shadows don't talk! But you don't say no to the mayor. By the third visit, *I'm* the one who knocks, presenting myself and then "my colleague."

I think you've gotten the hang of it, he says, even though I want to turn myself into his lapel pin and tag along for another gazillion visits at least. Our walk back to the chaplaincy offices is again paved with friendly interludes, *how are the kids* and *is your ankle better* and *I'll pick up the shoes from you this afternoon.* When I praise the mayor's ability to foster such deep rapport with staff so time-strapped that bathroom breaks are a luxury, he says only, *let the glory go to God, let the glory go to God.*

REMEMBER, OUR SUPERVISORS REMIND US, *the patients aren't here to see you.*

The staff chaplain whose church is a farmer's market* tells us, *Don't take it personally if they don't want you there. Or if they do want you there.*

One of the oncology nurses is a cancer survivor who can't imagine working on any other unit, though it breaks her heart every time she loses a patient. She sees her work as a gift, even when it leaves her bereft. There's a hint of Ulysses butterfly in her, black and blue, brilliant and bruised. The butterfly nurse informs me, *I don't want to talk to just anyone, I want to talk to* you.

The line between reliability and dependency is thin. The structure of our program is such that we will only be at the hospital one year. We arrive, we care, we rely and are relied on, we leave, we let go, we move on. Hubris and sanctimony are not what people need from chaplains.† There is an art to accepting compliments—and also a danger in falling for flattery's siren song.

Don't take it personally. Let the glory go elsewhere, to Guanyin or God, gumption or gratitude. A regular visitor (frequent flier, super utilizer, euphemistic labels for complicated circumstances) sings our praises every time he avails himself of chaplaincy services on his habitual trips to the ER. 24-7, 365, call the pager and a chaplain will come. He gushes, "You guys don't have to be here—but you're always here. You're, like, bonus, you know? Bonus like cream in coffee, like"—he searches for a better analogy—"like fried chicken!"

That day I'm a crispy drumstick. Another day I'm a guardian angel to a man who wants to drink a liter of Sprite, a man who is almost crying with thirst, a man who insists I *must. not. leave* (apparently one of the requisites of guardian angelship). With his nurse's permission, I steady the pitcher and guide the straw as fizzy bubbles leap up to tickle his nose hairs. Eventually I bid him goodbye, despite his heartrending pleas that I stay, stay. I'm sorry, I can't stay forever. I am no seraph.

You are learning your limits and generosities. Hearing these words from a college classmate, I nearly weep with relief. Permission to fall short of limitless generosity. I am no bodhisattva.

---

* Let us welcome our newest member, cara cara. Turn and greet your neighbor: why hello there, kohlrabi!

† Sometimes they just want to talk about killing large reptiles

EMAIL GREETING FROM A CLASSMATE at the Buddhist college in Taiwan:

菩薩你好!

Translation: *Hello, bodhisattva!*

I DO NOT HAVE HIGH HOPES for this visit.

The patient is Chinese American, a retired physician dying of leukemia. She commands us to call her "doctor," neutering any attempts to be on a first-name basis with her. The nurses plead with me to visit. Their interactions with the octogenarian have not been pleasant.

Today she is slumped in a chair, head lolled back, pearly skin belying her eighty-eight years. Her bedside tray holds a forlorn meal of mushy brown rice, oil-crusted soup, dried-out salmon, gloopy dessert. A shelf in the corner hosts an incongruously merry assortment of teddy bears, orchids, and get-well cards (behold: a puppy captioned "Sorry your tail's been drooping a little").

Every cell in my body is screaming to run out of the room.

"Dr. L, I wanted to check in to see how you are doing today . . ." I manage to choke out.

"Can't you see I'm miserable?" she snaps.

I try mirroring. "You're miserable. Is it ok if I pull up a chair?"

No response. I consider leaving, but the staff's desperation presses me on. I pull up a chair.

"Your nurses are quite concerned about you. Would you be willing to share a bit more about how you're feeling?"

"Like I said, I'm miserable. I keep gagging on my food. I haven't eaten for days." She closes her eyes.

I try paraphrasing. "That sounds really frustrating. I'm hearing that you've been trying to eat but that it's been very difficult."

She nods, eyes still closed, then takes the suction tube and sticks it down her throat. The clear fluid turns pink. A chunk of salmon rockets up the tube with a loud *schloop*.

I tell her it pains me to see her suffering and ask if there's anything that brings her comfort or relief. "The suctioning," she finally answers.

I venture a question about her religious beliefs. "You either have a religious tradition or you don't," she barks, refusing to elaborate further.

I attempt to gauge her sources of support. "I notice you have a lot of get-well cards and gifts . . ." She gives me a no-shit-Sherlock glare. My chair feels like it's on fire.

Sometimes silence ripens into intimacy. This time it ferments into hostility.

She opens her eyes a crack. "You're just sitting there like a vampire." Chagrined, I respond, "That sounds very distressing—I don't want to add to your suffering." She spits back, "Well you are!"

Whose need? our head supervisor asks when I present a verbatim* of the visit.

Oh. I see.

I took the words of the nurses too literally. In fixating on the target of their worries, I neglected to tend to the source of their distress. It was the nurses who needed a chaplain, not the patient. The dour doctor had a right to her rage, but there was no need to invite her invective, to play the balloon to her darts.

The next time I'm back on the unit, I commiserate with the nurses. Yes, it would be nicer for us if she were less ornery. But it's not Dr. L's job to wag her tail for us. We can't always get the happily ever after we want.

Some stories are not about transformation. Some visits suck the life out of everyone involved.

---

* *Verbatim:* (in)famous CPE assignment and educational tool. Reconstruct a visit on paper (dialogue, gestures, feelings—spare no detail). Answer a long series of questions about the visit. Present this verbatim to your peer group for feedback. Who knew the road to professional chaplaincy would be paved with amateur playwriting?

FIVE YEARS BEFORE I BECAME a fearsome fanged creature, a heavenly winged cherub, a delicious battered fowl, I was CHENXING—CHAPLAINCY INTERN at another hospital. In the trail of breadcrumbs that led me to CPE, those few months of volunteering two nights a week could easily form a half loaf.

The harried and hardworking staff like to say that this San Francisco community hospital is "as real as it gets." In nervous imitation of the harried and hardworking staff, I hurry down the halls. Then I remember our supervisor's credo: The chaplain's role is the opposite of fitting in. While others rush to meet quotas, we pause to make space. What the medical system sees as failure—dying, death—we understand as ineluctable and sacred. When others flee the room, we enter.

I slow my steps.

Hi, my name is Chenxing and I'm from the chapla—"No English!" The first patient I visit is Chinese. My Mandarin falters as I try to explain my role. I finally glom onto a word I used in China during my gap year, when I taught English in Shanghai: 义工. It becomes my fallback, this generic term for *volunteer,* its simplified version requiring just six brush strokes (义工), its vagueness a blank canvas for all kinds of projections.

My second visit is with a Russian woman. "Volunteer" appears to be in her English vocabulary. "Chaplain" is not. I help her adjust the uncooperative plastic arm that attaches a tiny TV to her hospital bed. "Junk," she declares. She's right. Channels 22 to 64 are snowy static. To be at face level with her in a room without chairs, I kneel on the cold linoleum, anchored and penitent. "God bless you," she says as our brief visit draws to a close. "Do you want to pray?" I blurt out. This is before I learn that chaplaincy visits do not need to follow a formula, that prayer can be welcome or dreaded, exultant or desultory, apropos or dispensable. Bemused, she mutters something to the effect of *I don't actually believe in God; I just like to say God bless you.*

The third visit is with a Filipina woman whose bulletin board hosts a panoply of Jesuses and Marys. She wants to know how China compares to the Philippines (how is the food? the weather? the corruption?). She tells me about her adult children and teenage grandson and her belief in one God looking over us all. "Can we pray?" she asks. Sometimes, prayer brings closure. Other times, it offers an opening. After we pray, she cries. "I was ready to die," she confides. But it was a miracle, the surgery wasn't needed after all. "Give me a hug," she insists, her embrace a fond farewell.

More visits follow. A Spanish-speaking woman beset by an aneurysm. An older white man, formerly incarcerated, now living on the streets. A young Black man with metal rods in his leg after a motorcycle accident.

At the threshold of each patient's room, I can foresee nothing of the visit ahead. This not-knowing is terrifying. It asks me: What if chaplaincy wasn't just what you did in the interstices of three part-time jobs? What would happen if you gave it your undivided attention for a full year?

ONCE, WALKING THROUGH THE WOODS, the Buddhist boyfriend and I come across—well actually, we have no idea what it is. Half-asleep, chubby-cheeked, barrel-bodied, mouse-eared, bushy-tailed, guinea-pig-sized, scintillant-furred, unfazed creature. The first phrase that comes to my mind is "exploding cancerous muskrat." T agrees it looks bloated. Where did it come from? What should we do?

Lacking the wherewithal (ok, nerve) to capture this unearthly critter, we drive to the nearby nature education center. The blurry photo on my Wi-Fi-less flip phone only generates flummoxed looks. Just then, sudden as a sneeze, memory strikes. The college friend who managed to smuggle rabbits into her dorm room—what she really wanted was an animal I'd never heard of before. South American. Bathes in dust. Jumps six feet high. Could it be? A chinchilla? The image slowly loads on the nature center computer.

Bingo. We have found a chinchilla, a 龙猫, a dragon cat, a Totoro. (In my favorite scene from the movie, the titular character dances a whole forest into existence. In Cambodia, deprived of the self-care essential of vitamin tree, I will yearn for this dense lushness.)

T and I page through the phone book, looking for the nearest animal shelters. *Beeeeeep. You've reached Wuuuuundu and Steve's Raaaabbit Rescue.* A drawling voice explains that they only take rabbits. The nearest humane society won't take this chinchilla either, though for reasons of geography rather than species: since we're technically in an unincorporated area of the adjacent county, we'll need to drive forty-five minutes north to the animal shelter there.

But first, how do we capture this guy? The nature center volunteer digs a cardboard box out of the recycling. We toss it in the trunk and drive back to the trail. The chinchilla hasn't budged. Not bloated or dying after all, just domesticated and crepuscular, sleepy at this non-dusk-non-dawn hour. We attempt to coax it into the box. Whiskers twitching, the chinchilla hops everywhere but in. I concede that it's pretty cute, though I remain too afraid to touch. (Inner catastrophist: what if rabies?) Fingers curled awkwardly (but protectively!) into my armpit, I poke feebly in its general direction with a limp coat sleeve.

We spot a ranger on break—fortunately, he seems to have missed my (futile) one-winged chicken dance. Rushing over, I beg, Oliver Twist–like,

Please, sir, could we have some food, just a morsel, anything will do? The ranger raises a quizzical eyebrow, decides he's better off not asking, and hands over his snack. The sunflower seeds do the trick. Into the box the chinchilla goes. After a few energetic thumps against the hastily closed lid, the furry fellow dozes off once more.

At the humane society, the volunteers can barely contain themselves. They grab the chinchilla and smother her with kisses.

Hmm. Guess that settles any doubts about how dangerous she is.

The volunteers are eager to educate us about chinchillas. Did you know they're hypoallergenic? (That's good news, since T is allergic to cats.) Do you want to adopt it? You have first dibs since you found her! (We're momentarily tempted.) They can live twenty years, you know. (Uhh, nix the adoption papers.) Feel the fur, feel the fur! Fifty hairs a follicle!

I feel. There is almost no difference between where air ends and chinchilla begins.

THE NEXT TIME I MEET a chinchilla is in the 16th arrondissement of Paris. The scarf in the window display snakes around a number whose head is a euro sign and whose tail has too many zeros. When recognition dawns, I hurry past with a shudder, bile in my throat.

Maybe the vampire-dreading doctor was crepuscular, and we kept catching her at a bad time. Maybe she'd been abandoned. Maybe she was softer than we thought. Maybe the fear was all in my head.

THE MORE SUFFERING, THE BETTER. Chaplaincy, life: hard when you're in it, but then you look back and find the lessons and gifts . . .

Separated from his parents during the war, the reverend-to-be receives a concerned letter from his mother. He begins to write a response but is too ashamed of his childish Japanese to continue.

He crumples his sorry start of a letter into the wastebin, not knowing his mother will die waiting for that discarded response. Decades later, the reverend will reread the last letter his mother sent. For the first time, he will notice the blots on the onionskin paper. The places where her tears had fallen.

MY FATHER ONCE SAID THAT his biggest regret about leaving China was that I would never get to know my grandparents. And not just grandparents. Aunties and uncles and cousins, the firsts- and seconds-, greats- and great-greats, twice- and thrice-removeds. All rendered strangers by a single one-way flight.

On the trip over, I wouldn't stop playing hide-and-seek with my increasingly stressed-out father. By then, my mother had already been in the US for nearly a year, which amounted to almost a quarter of my life, though I remember neither her absence nor our reunion.

Apparently, my favorite part of this new country was the fried chicken. But after the first week, I never ate with such gusto again. Not fried chicken. Not anything.

ARRIVING IN AMERICA INAUGURATED ME to fear.

Of not understanding a word of the language. Which, at first, I did not.

Of not fitting in, at school or outside of it. Which the things cast my way— pebbles and *ching-chongs* and wide-eyes-pulled-slant—suggested I did not.

Of not knowing how to fend for myself. Which I mitigated by memorizing my Social Security number and filling in the ledger lines of a checkbook that accounted for every found penny, copper coins scavenged from dusty corners where aliens like me could hide, out of range of stones and singsongs and open-eyes-pulled-squint.

How to describe this newfound fear? It's not the kind you get from encountering loud thunder or mean dogs, but something quieter and heavier and far more treacherous, the kind of fear that is inseparable from existential dread. A miasma stubborn to lift, sensed only by you.

DEAREST,

From your hospital room in Portland, you wrote: "When you feel yourself working hard to worry . . ."

I am far too good at working hard in this regard. I wish I could be like the youngest of your two older brothers. Utterly unworried when your mom happened upon the large snake that had taken up residence under his bed. Your brother who was always forgetting to close the screen door between his bedroom and the backyard. The snake, cozy among crumpled socks, looked like it had been there for months.

My writing desk is surrounded by quotes you've given me over the years. Like this one, nested inside a scratched black frame, about the noble art of leaving things undone

MY BIGGEST FEAR IN THIRD grade is that my dad will die in a car accident on the way home from work. In an age before cell phones, many a 6 p.m. finds me nervously eyeing the clock. The minutes tick past. I remain decidedly alone in the apartment.

My parents are separated by their jobs, I dutifully inform the requisite adults (in retrospect, all white women) at my school, but the way their narrowed eyes don't match the *Sure, honey,* that comes out of their mouths tells me I am suspect.

Maryland (capital: Annapolis), Virginia (Richmond), North Carolina (Raleigh), South Carolina (Columbia), Georgia (Atlanta), oh, yes, and Washington, D.C. (that one's easy) separate me from my mom. I'm the only student whose mom is absent from our Mother's Day celebration. At the afternoon ceremony, I bestow my macaroni art and school-issued carnation upon a phantom. The carnation rots long before I see my mom next.

By 6:07 p.m., I am convinced my father is dead inside a totaled Nissan and my mother will not want me burdening her faraway life. In college, the Buddhist boyfriend will tell me that the Cambodian word for orphan, ក្មេងកំព្រា, includes those who have lost just one parent. This definition will make complete sense.

Mom is definitely the better cook. Dad has lately developed a penchant for sauerkraut and boiled lettuce, so-called foods that the word *gross* was clearly invented to define. In the fridge is a cabbage awaiting its krauted fate. In the pantry is a pack of dried jellyfish, nothing like the exotic and immediately edible Doritos and Oreos at my (white) gal pals' homes.

By 6:09 p.m., even butter cannot soothe me. Butter is how I allay my lonely hunger in the late afternoons. I shear the yellowish stick with the edge of a fork because the only knife in sight is a cleaver too heavy for me to lift. I put the jagged sliver on my tongue like a priest I once saw. He was administering wafers. Even then, I knew the host was not meant for my (heathen) kind.

When I hear the click of the lock at 6:13 p.m., I run to the bathroom to splash cold water on my face. Wash off the tears and snot. Pigtails askew, no time to adjust. Paper on a smile. Greet my father.

Chaplaincy will make me remember these moments. Will make me wish I could reach into the papery past and tell that pigtailed girl what my supervisors say to me: *It's ok to cry in front of others. The truth deepens relationships.*

M HAS OUTLIVED HER PROGNOSIS by three weeks already. "I guess that means we can't know what things will be like three weeks from now," she muses.

This must be my seventh or eighth visit to her hospital room. "How is your spirit today?" I ask.

M smiles at the familiar question. "Normally I feel like Eeyore, but today— today I feel more like Pooh. Pooh is more hopeful." On an earlier visit, we'd gotten to talking about our favorite inhabitants of the Hundred Acre Wood after M, vexed about who would care for her cat, had sighed, "Oh, bother."

I see why today is a Pooh day. Her daughter, D, is flying in from halfway across the globe. M hasn't seen D since she moved overseas with her husband and their babies. The little ones will be staying with M's mom. D is afraid for them to see Grandma, whose cancer has made her look even older than Great-Gran.

M knows this will be her last visit with her daughter. "I hope they'll be ok when I'm gone," she murmurs.

On Eeyore days, God feels distant. On Eeyore days, M laments her timid life of unfulfilled dreams. How she never made it to Istanbul. Never opened that antique shop. Didn't make more time—and now she's too weak—to read the books she loves by those women who get right to the marrow of the bone.

On Piglet days, she ventures a tiny dream: to go home, drink juice, sit in the sun, pet her cat who likes to hide M's glasses in the water dish.

D visits daily until the time comes for her to return to Istanbul. She is sitting in a chair by the hospital bed when I stop by on their last day together. I ask M what she has liked most about her daughter's visit.

She looks embarrassed.

I give her time. By this final month of my CPE residency, silence has become both cherished tool and comforting companion, even if vampire accusations might lie on the other end.

Finally, M whispers, "The times when we just sit and hold hands. But I keep thinking, maybe I shouldn't reach for my daughter's hand."

"Oh, mom . . ."

When she's flustered, M tends to change the subject. "What time is your flight, honey? Are you all packed up? What about—"

"*Mom!* Stop worrying about me, we need to be taking care of *you.* You know I want to stay longer but I can't have other people taking care of my kids forever!" D shrinks back in her chair after this outburst.

I know too well this dance of raised hackles and withdrawn hearts. I grab M's right hand in my left and D's left hand in my right. I squeeze, hard.

I let them break the silence.

"I don't want to cry because I don't want to upset you," D confesses.

"I cry too, when you're not here," M admits.

D's laugh cracks with incredulity and relief. "I guess we're trying to be strong for each other."

I unite their hands and remove mine. I know they're afraid to cry. They know it's ok to cry. The moment their hands touch, the worrying words short-circuit. The moment their hands touch, everything is ok. Their hands touching is cat and sun and juice and home, bittersweet, home.

AS IS PROBABLY THE CASE for every Chinese kid ever, the first snake-related 成语 I learned was 画蛇添足. As with every four-character idiom, *Draw a snake and add feet to it* is a *chengyu* with a backstory.

Long ago, in the state of 楚 *(770–223 BC, around present-day* 湖北*), someone who's just finished making offerings to the ancestors has a jug of wine he's looking to give away. It's ample wine for one person, but hardly enough to go around. The solution? A contest: whoever can draw a snake the fastest gets the jug. In a flash, the figure of a snake emerges in front of the speediest illustrator. He's got one hand on the jug and one eye on his slower opponents when he hesitates—why not spruce up the picture a bit, he's got time, his other hand's free. Embellishments added, he's about to chug the wine when another guy, snake completed, steals the prize. Whoever saw a snake with feet, man? the johnny-come-lately crows, gulping down his reward.*

Though our Chinese teacher edited out the booze when she taught us the story.

IF 画蛇添足 IS A CAUTIONARY tale about overdoing it, the moral was completely lost on me.

On the last day of sixth grade, my teacher pulls me aside. She's about to congratulate me, I'm sure of it. My grades never deviate from the first letter of the alphabet. If an assignment calls for two pages, I turn in twelve.

You can't keep doing this. Her stern voice explodes my anticipatory pride into shards of shame. *You can't work this hard. You are going to burn out.*

My lips tighten across metal braces. I want to scream, *This is how I've survived the never-ending disorientation, the move from China to America, the move from school to school to school to school to this school, with a new school on the horizon next year, each time a whole new set of faces—this is the only way I know to be someone.* I taste the blood in my mouth and say nothing.

Time will prove her right, of course. It's a survival strategy that will nearly kill me.

SEVENTEEN YEARS AFTER MY SIXTH-GRADE teacher's warning, one of my CPE supervisors looks me in the eye and declares: "You have a tendency to overdo it."

This time, I hear the care in her words. This time, I laugh in recognition.

MY BIGGEST FEAR AS A chaplain is that I am not enough.

It's a posture of flinching. Awaiting punishment for my failure to measure up to the ideal (white Buddhist? Black Christian?) chaplain.

It's a posture of hiding. An elephant inside a snake, masquerading as a hat, the smallness and stillness a feint.

Maybe it's true, $I \neq enough$, when $I \neq everything$, when I is not even an identifiable *any*thing.

But why must one need everything to be enough?

If I needs everything to be enough, there will never be enough, just a bottomless chasm of insatiable need.

My father was born in a famine year. Unlike his less fortunate compatriots, he and I have never known hunger.

Sometimes, though, I feel I have never known anything except hunger.

Exhibit 1: As a days-old infant, I eat so much and so often that my mother feeds me formula and sugar water to spare her chafed nipples.

Exhibit 2: At the age of four, I develop a habit of circling the adults' chairs after I've already eaten at the kids' table. Saucers for eyes, mouth open wide, I wait for morsels like a ravenous but obedient dog. The pointy ends of chopsticks regard me with suspicion. *Are you* really *not full yet?* Sucking in my chubby stomach, I nod vigorously.

Exhibit 3: All that fried chicken, the first week in America.

IN COLLEGE I WILL LEARN words that strip *want* and *hunger* to the core. *Tanha* and *dukkha,* craving like an unquenchable thirst, dissatisfactoriness like a cart's off-kilter wheel.

Exhibit A: At the age of four, when our neighbor asks if I would like a snack, I politely request 三个毛豆, which will do nothing to allay my hunger but—crucially—will not be an imposition. The little girl who limited her wanting to exactly three furry green soybean pods will circulate in neighborhood lore long after she's gone.

Exhibit B: In first grade, a twenty-dollar bill, folded in eighths and tucked into a manila envelope the size of a business card, pays for a month of subsidized school breakfasts and lunches. One month, I lose the envelope. Despite my panic, I resolve to carry out the only solution. I will hide the loss. Forgo a month of foil-wrapped meals. Feign fullness.

Exhibit C: *I am losing my language.* The thought comes to me in English, in the same year that I lose the manila envelope, on an afternoon when I am home alone after school in an apartment where cockroaches dance on toothbrushes and ceiling rains snowmelt into kitchen pots. In front of me is a black vinyl notebook barely larger than the size of a business card, issued by the State Education Commission of the People's Republic of China, Nainai's gift to a granddaughter who is replacing her mother tongue at an inner-city school in Pittsburgh. I want to record the events of the day in my native language, but when I look at the page, there are only shaky characters and sentences full of holes. Their monstrosity sears me with the horrible truth. If the most hideous of ducklings can no longer sustain a delusion of swanhood, would she not flee her reflection like her very life depends on it? I tear out the repulsive pages and shove the wadded paper into the wastebasket.

I still have that mutilated notebook, ragged edges where the missing pages once held on. Chaplaincy will make me remember those pages. Will make me wish I had fished those tearstained papers out of the garbage, had unwrinkled them and given myself back to myself. If someone had told me that throwing something away doesn't mean you'll forget it, doesn't mean you won't miss it, would I still be here now, searching for the irretrievable, striving for an impossible perfection?

AT THE FINAL MONTHLY MEETING of the introduction to Buddhist chaplaincy training program, one of our teachers looks us in the eye and declares: *Chaplaincy works better if the chaplain is imperfect.*

杯弓蛇影: ANOTHER SNAKE-RELATED CHENGYU WITH a boozy backstory.

Long ago, during the Jin Dynasty (AD 265–420), a man with a fondness for lavish parties is throwing one at his house. As drink and conversation flow freely around them, he offers a goblet of wine to his friend. Whereupon the friend spots a small snake swimming inside the goblet. The terrified guest downs the contents of the goblet and immediately excuses himself. (Apparently, imbibing a serpent is preferable to being a party pooper.) After days of seeing neither hide nor hair of his friend, our baffled host tracks the man down, only to discover that his pal has been deathly ill since the night of the party. When the ailing man divulges the cause of his malady, he's coaxed back to the room where he quaffed the serpent-laced wine. Et voilà: a hunting bow hangs on the wall. The swimming snake was merely the shadow of the 弓 reflected in the goblet.

Four years before buying a one-way ticket to Taiwan, I visit the island country for the first time. After attending the Buddhist studies conference that brought us there, the Buddhist boyfriend and I take the long route—via Keelung, Hualien, Kaohsiung, and Taipei—to our next destinations of Bangkok (where I'll be attending a Buddhist women's conference) and Siem Reap (where a Khmer studies conference awaits). At Jinguashih, we gravitate not toward the remnants of the town's past (copper and gold mines, prisoner-of-war camp) but to the rampant foliage that encroaches on this history with heliotropic heedlessness. Looking down the ravine at a canopy-carpet of every imaginable shade of green, my companion lets out a shout. An enormous green snake!

It's as if that ravine is the goblet in 杯弓蛇影 writ large. Is there a snake? Is there not? A few passersby pause to take a look before continuing on unfazed. They either don't see it or aren't too worked up about it.

PART III: 半梦半醒

dreaming awake

"THIS USED TO BE A MENTAL INSTITUTION," a Chinese nun informs me on my first visit to her Buddhist community in Northern California.

She pauses, a hint of mischief in her voice.

"Maybe it still is."

DAAA-DAAA-DAAAA!

I jolt at the pager's shrill beep. It's the inpatient psychiatric facility paging. I'm the twenty-four-hour on-call chaplain today. Everyone else in the spiritual care department has gone home for the evening, so this call is for me.

After the three-mile drive north from The Tower, after the safekeeping of my belongings in a numbered locker, I enter empty-handed through the first set of double doors, wait for them to clank closed before walking through the second set, and come face-to-face with a Vietnamese American teenager.

In her long black hair and sad steely eyes, I see a vision of myself at her age, dictating suicide letters into the night.

She tells me she is Buddhist. She's surprised to find out that we've both spent time at the same Buddhist community in the hills of Northern California. We speak of survival in this mad, mad world. I want her to see *Wong Flew Over the Cuckoo's Nest,* to know there are routes to freedom—if she can stay alive to traverse them.

The next week, back at The Tower, I meet a Sino-Vietnamese man old enough to be the teenage girl's father. *I'm going crazy with insomnia,* he says, his face an anguished plea. *Sometimes it's so bad I want to die.*

No one in his household believes him. Humbug, they say. How is it possible to be unable to sleep? You fled from Vietnam to China in the '70s—how could a little lost sleep possibly be worse than losing your home? You managed to immigrate from China to this Promised Land in the '90s—the hardship is past, is it not?

The stab of family refusing to listen. In third grade, insomnia plagues me for weeks on end. The terror of those lightless hours chases me down the hallway to the other bedroom door, where my piteous mewling wakes up my parents. 我睡不着，我睡不着 . . . They are not amused. *What the heck's wrong with you? Just go back to sleep. And close the damn door on your way out!*

Another Vietnamese patient in The Tower lives alone and works as a waiter at a casino. He says with a shrug that he is schizophrenic and no saint. Life is simple: salary gets reinvested in the slot machines, city of gambles offers food and friends to boot, sister pays for his apartment. He worries his buddies have missed him. He never misses a day of work if he can help it.

A few days later I see him waiting at the curb, still shaky but cleared to leave. His sister pulls up in a Benz. Bedecked in gold and wrapped in furs, she stares resolutely ahead, manicured fingers tapping the steering wheel, mouth a grim line. The passenger door is still half open as the Mercedes speeds off.

The hospital is full of madness and dreams. Outside the hospital is no different.

A WOMAN WHOSE HUSBAND IS drinking himself to death is sure this time will be like all the others. Sure he will leave the ICU alive, like always.

"It was not the life I imagined," she tells me in Chinese, without bitterness. She smooths her hair, rubs the hem of her dress, taps her knee.

Her husband has always supported—no, *supports*—her art. He has always loved—no, *loves*—their boys.

Her hand is a restless bird, seeking its familiar calligraphy brush perch.

We see 酒鬼, a neglectful father and failing organ systems.

She sees 愛人, her doting lover and hope against the odds.

She is 盼望, we are 失望. Shall I enter her hope? Dare I defy it? Will it change the calculus of her heart if we are right and he never goes home again?

A YOUNG MAN INVITES ME to sit across from his hospital bed. He has beautiful hazel eyes, a presence that glows, a recent HIV diagnosis. He wants, like James Baldwin, to go to Europe. Last night a dream whisked him to heaven, where everything was white and gold, pearly gates sun-saturated.

Two years later, walking in Paris, I come across an elephant. Not the gentle gray giant who roamed the streets of Phnom Penh among tuk-tuks and motorbikes on my first trip to Cambodia, but one of his kin, immortalized in photograph, standing on a beach in Sri Lanka, colors so muted the whole scene takes on the quality of reverie.

Asleep in her hospital bed one evening not long before I left for France, my former roommate dreamt of a white elephant that bathed her in peace and lovingkindness. She awoke feeling protected. *Everything will be ok.*

I know where this poster needs to be. The young man who captured the image of this Sri Lankan elephant is on lunch break. His girlfriend, also a photographer, takes my euros and wraps the rolled-up print in a thick bundle of newspaper. On my quest to buy a mailing tube, the print slips out onto the cobblestone alleys of the Jewish Quarter. I retrace my steps in a panic. Two blocks back, I find the elephant half-unfurled on the sidewalk.

I eat lunch late that day. Afterward, pain seizes my gut, turning my steps into limps. I lie down on a park bench, figuring I can sleep it off, to no avail. Groaning, I retrace the many miles back to the hotel, arriving at nightfall. For months, the pain flares and abates, never fully leaving. I try all sorts of elimination diets, to no avail. I can rid my meals of gluten and yeast, wheat and FODMAPs. But grief—grief will not be spurned.

TROUBLE BREWING: THE HOSPITAL STAFF are split among those who believe the boy and those who see an incorrigible opportunist. Unlike the rescued chinchilla, his arrival is not met with unmitigated glee.

The boy's medical records don't add up. There is no scientific explanation for the level of pain he claims to be in. There is speculation that he has lied about his age and is actually a minor.

With some he is compliant,* that much-lauded trait of model patients. Sweet as a suckling babe.

With others he is combative, a storm of curses and complaint. A fury that will not be contained.

Somewhere between complaint and compliance is a life I want to live.

A psychologist weighs in with a special DSM diagnosis that cautions us against this pathological manipulator.

The boy wants to read scripture. I give him a red Bible. He clutches it like a flotation device.

He tells me about his father who died young, but not before buying a house and new car for his family. He tells me he's afraid of needles, because when he was six he woke up to see one sticking out of his brother's limp body. His mother? "I'm glad she's not psychotic anymore. Other people say she's crazy, but I don't think so."

The nurses are fed up with their youngest patient's inconsistent stories and too-consistent demands for painkillers and pantry snacks.

---

* The word always sounds warped to my ear, as if the hospital is an arena for best in show.

MY SECOND-GRADE TEACHER IN PITTSBURGH made each of us keep a journal. Mine opens with the news that my father is going to Ohio for three weeks before heading to "Marryland."

I write: "Some times my father only comes on Saturdays because he will need to move somewhere to another house and if he come home then he cannot move to other contrys." (Apparently, I have not yet mastered the distinction between apartments and houses, states and countries.)

I write: "When my mother finish her job me and my mother can go to China." (No, we couldn't possibly have had the money or the visas to do that.)

In my father's absence, I weave fantastical stories about his whereabouts. With my weak grasp of geography and weaker handle on grown-up affairs, I improvise, crafting the stories from whatever's on hand. Like the cranes we make after school from begged scraps of paper at the Carnegie Library.* Like the ladder we build from pieces of string surreptitiously slipped off stacks of newspaper at the university across the street.†

---

* The librarian waits in vain for us to request a call number on one of those slips.

† Roaming the college halls, four seven-year-old Chinese girls perfect this art: wait until the coast is clear, beeline to the tightly bound block of papers, shimmy off the string without tearing the edges of the newsprint—et voilà, the perfect loop for cat's cradle.

"I FEEL REALLY BEAT UP today," groans one of our youngest doctors as he reviews the mystery patient's files.

It doesn't feel good to be used: the ego protests.

Plumb the depths of anyone and you'll find more than meets the eye.

Is he a nefarious con artist, living off the taxpayer dollar, feigning pain to munch graham crackers and mainline opioids?

Is he just a kid with real pain of phantom origins, a child who misses his father and only wants to be heard, a homeless young man whose final recourse is to build his palaces in hospital rooms across the country?

Questions pile upon questions. Answers prove more and more elusive.

Is this a case of embellishing the truth? Overdosing on myth? A fairy tale grim?

Would it make a difference if he believed his own stories? If there was no kingly father or uncrazed mother or long-dead brother, but he was convinced otherwise?

Clever or criminal? Boy or man? Sensitive suffering prince or royal pain in the ass?

Would we treat him differently if he was not Black?

This house of mirrors: carnival game or minotaur's lair? What's at stake, fun or survival?

How many tales have I engineered to garner sympathy?

Can we ever untangle our stories from our dreams?

EVERYONE HAS AN OPINION. I am hooked too. Do we take the patient at face value, or suspect the holes in his story? Several days pass. He says his pain is only getting worse, despite the raft of pain meds he's on. Is this a spiderweb of deception, with only the mastermind spinner unstuck?

The first brahmavihara: immeasurable lovingkindness. Mindstate sublime. Dwelling divine. It is possible to wish someone well even if you think they are your enemy. Even if you don't like them. Even if you don't believe them.

A fellow chaplain resident scribbles in the margins of my verbatim: *unicorn?*

I DON'T KNOW IF I will have children. If I do, I don't know what stories or contrys they will inhabit—but I hope they believe that every situation, no matter how intractable, holds the possibility of connection.

The young man asks for a prayer. We pray.

The next day, he's gone. Walked to the bus stop. Rode on to his next destination. And the debilitating leg pain?

A few years later, a friend will say to me, with utmost love, *there is no need to police other people's integrity.*

I wish him well, that unicorn of a boy who flummoxed us all.

ANOTHER WAKING DREAM:

One of our patients has stayed on the medical/renal unit more than half a year already. She has two monikers, a given name and a nickname. I call her by the latter.

Hospitals are designed for acute care, not long-term stays. "When can I go home?" K asks every time I see her. This time is no different.

We go for our routine walk-and-talk around the sixth floor.

The identities of her family members—mother, father, aunt, three sons— have slithered away from her. Where are they now, I ask? I don't know, she replies cheerfully, furrowing her brow to conjure only: *mom, dad, auntie, my boys*. K never remembers my name, but sometimes she intercepts me in the hallway to ask for a prayer.

Despite multiple social workers' tireless efforts, none of the nursing homes within a hundred-mile radius are willing to accept her. They add up how much she will cost over the course of her life. K has lost her memory but not her robustness. She looks healthy, is even putting on weight. She is not likely to die anytime soon. Gears grind, a cash register pings. She will be a burden for decades. Her discharge date* is forever pending, pending, pending.

To combat the languor of K's bardos-long stay in a room that can never become a long-term home, one of the social workers arranges for an exercise bike. A rainbow cursor spins on a computer that has met the incalculable. K can cycle off the calories, but she can't cycle out of limbo.

---

* Why is medicalese so ugly, as if the ultimate goal is expulsion and not healing?

MENTAL STATUS EXAM. IS SHE oriented to person, place, time, and situation? On the rare occasions when K passes, it is never with flying colors. One day I watch a doctor declare that an elderly Chinese patient is not oriented to time because she can't tell him her birth year. But she is thinking in animals (horses, tigers, monkeys) and not numbers (1942, 1950, 1944). Another day I read in the chart of a Cambodian patient that his primary language is Cantonese (it's not). At a friend's house in San Francisco, during a fundraising dinner for a South African nonprofit, a Frenchman asks where I'm from and interrupts me mid-sentence to remark, "but you all look the same!" (we don't).

If the test-givers are dubiously oriented, can we really pass judgment on the test-takers?

TODAY THOUGH, BEYOND A SHADOW of a doubt, I would fail that test. Barely oriented to person-place-time-situation after an intense twenty-four-hour on-call shift, I have eight more hours to endure before I can go home. When K appears by my side, it's all I can do not to lean on her. Were it not for my badge and her gown, you would think she was the chaplain.

Round and round we go, in clockwise circumambulations, as if the center nursing station is something sacred. Walking meditation, she in closed-toe shoes, me in sock-padded feet—no, sorry, the other way around.

"What did you dream about last night?" I ask K. She tries hard to remember.

I don't usually volunteer much information about myself.* I don't like to shift the focus away from my conversation partner. But today, sleep-deprived and shaken from the drama of the previous evening's on-call shift, I tell K about a recurring dream of mine. In the dream, I am euphoric. The coins I've found are shiny and rare enough to rival the one's in my mother's collection. Best of all, they are *mine*, finders keepers. I can't wait to show her, to see the expression—jealous? congratulatory?—on my mother's face. Every time, I wake up with empty hands, flooded with loss and shame.

K responds with a numismatic story of her own. "My father used to have coins all around the house. Jars and jars full of them. There were four of us. We would add coins to the jars too. Although sometimes we would try to take coins out too, I don't remember for what, maybe lunch money?"

We complete our fourth lap. "Oh! I think this is my room!" K points to the door marked by a sheet of printer paper with a hand-drawn star on it. Hollywood meets HIPAA, an anonymous pentagram.

Wish upon a star to find your way home. My walking companion is 没头脑 without the 不高兴. My favorite story as a child: 没头脑和不高兴, Forgetful (aka No-Brains) and I-Don't-Wanna (aka Unhappy). *Read it again,*

---

* In the unmoored time after Nainai's death, before my sojourn as chaplaincy intern at the as-real-as-it-gets hospital, I signed up for another volunteer spiritual care program. I almost made it to the end of orientation. What did me in: Shadowing a garrulous volunteer for a seemingly interminable two-hour shift. "*My* husband had multiple-bypass surgery too! Let me tell you, it was a *real* headache for me. . . ."

read it again, I beg my mom, the book holy in my hands, one of the few possessions we brought to America, carefully protected by a homemade forest green cover made from an advertisement for collet chucks from the Shanghai No. 1 Machine Tool Accessory Factory. *Again, again,* I beg my mom, until she becomes 不高兴 and refuses to read on, snapping *What kind of* 没头脑 *can't read this stupid story themselves?*

Standing next to the starred room, K tries to recall what happened to her mother and sister. "I can't quite remember . . . I guess we all went our separate ways." A frown crosses her face but doesn't stay there for long. "Thank you for the walk. I really enjoyed it."

"Me too, K, me too." I'd needed that walk more than she could know. "Thank *you.*"

DEAR LOVE,

I think my dad would find the mercy in K's condition. Better 没头脑 than 不高兴, he would say.

不要想太多, he used to say to my furrowed brow, but of course I'd be doing just the opposite, dwelling and worrying and overthinking, even though he was right about this being a surefire recipe for unhappiness. Another of his dad-phorisms: 明天的事情明天再想. Worry about tomorrow tomorrow.

This is what you will write while undergoing chemo: "When you feel yourself working hard to worry, remember that it is okay to be just where you are and give yourself permission to embrace that."

THERE'S ANOTHER WOMAN ON THE same unit who has been here half as long as K, which is to say still a very long time. She too is young. She too is "a placement issue." Only, she's got tattoos of the names of her babies. If only K had done the same.

I have no babies whose names I can tattoo, but my family name is inked on my back, left of spine, just above my hip, where I forget its existence for years at a time. I have an imprint of this solitary stamp on a square of gauze, the dried blood showing the mirror image of a 韓 in seal script, inscribed in a circle whose circumference is interrupted by a cluster of three stars and a fourth larger star, the fourth star representing the uncle whose dying spurred my eighteen-year-old self to visit a tattoo parlor in my birthplace and his deathplace of Shanghai.

Some stories I'll never know the ending to. A library book unfinished, one that can't be borrowed again. Our resident star, in her bedroom/living room/ dressing room/gym, is still there when I graduate from CPE, still pedaling on her exercise bike, yearning to go home.

"BODHISATTVAS RESPOND TO OUR PRAYERS. To what extent do you agree with this statement?"

One of the Japanese American Shin Buddhists I interviewed suggests: All people can be bodhisattvas. And prayers don't have to be silent or private. So anytime you ask someone for help and receive it, a bodhisattva has just responded to your prayer!

How easy to make bodhisattvas of each other by this definition—and yet how hard too. Witness the group activity "Pathway to Success." Participants are blindfolded and their hands placed along a thick length of rope that has been draped over an elaborate obstacle course. Their objective is to feel their way to the exit. They can raise their hands for help at any point. It is an exercise in mounting frustration, because the course has no beginning and no end— the rope is one giant loop. The pathway to success? Raise your hand to ask for help, whereupon a volunteer will gently lead you away from the course and take off your blindfold. The savvy few watch in amusement as the rest of us grope clumsily on.

Can you guess how I fared? The only child, the latchkey kid, the girl who balanced her checkbook at the age of seven, the young woman who craved suicide as the coda to her imperfectible life.

My first time playing Pathway to Success, I cling stubbornly to that rope, refusing to believe I can't figure this out on my own.

The game can take a long, long time.

DÉJÀ VU: AS CHAPLAIN RESIDENTS, we always have the option of paging our supervisors for support. But I've been on call every week for nine months; we're graduating in two. That long, long evening, not once does the thought of asking for help ever cross my mind.

I have been paged by a nurse to come and support "a few distraught family members" for "a patient who is expiring." Upon arriving at the ICU, I realize that "a few" means about fifteen (how did they all fit into this tiny room?), "distraught" is code for complete pandemonium, and "expiring" can now be rendered in the past tense. It is like walking onto a stage where the apogees of a dozen gut-wrenching plays are happening simultaneously.

My first instinct is to flee. Two men stand dazed outside the door.

The nurse sees me and gasps with relief, "Oh good, you're the chaplain!"

I may have muttered "Oh, shit" under my breath at this point.

Inside the cramped room, men and women are crying, beating their bodies, stomping, howling, shouting in a language I will later learn is Tigre. Someone is thrashing around on the floor.

On the bed, a thin woman with braided hair is dead. Her neck is bent to the left. A thin line of blood trails from her mouth to the pillow. She looks younger than the age listed in her medical chart, so much so that I mistake one of her daughters for a sister. This daughter is screaming in rage, kicking the floor, being restrained by two family members. Another young woman leans against a dripping faucet, cradling her head, still as a statue. A third woman is pounding her chest and legs in a trance, chanting *oo-wee, oo-wee, oo-wee*—or is it *oh why, oh why, oh why*?

More family come. Fresh wails erupt. All around me people are moving and people are collapsing, people are hyperventilating and people are retching. The noise level is deafening.

Even the seasoned ICU nurses are panicked, tears pricking their eyes as they ask, "what should we do?" They beg me to calm everyone down. I am feeling inadequate, inadequate, inadequate.

In a room of chaos, one calm person makes a difference.

In a room of chaos, one calm person might not stay calm for long.

This might have been a good time to call in reinforcements.

One of the daughters gestures to me, then points at her mother's body. "Do you see her? She was the BEST MOTHER in the WORLD. WHY DID SHE HAVE TO DIE? WHY?!"

"What are your favorite memories of her?" As soon the words escape my mouth, I silently rebuke myself. This is a later question, not a now question. It's too soon. Later there will be time for remembrance. Now she is gripped in holy war with her mother's goneness.

"THERE ARE NO WORDS FOR MY MOTHER. NO WORDS!" she shrieks.

There is no fairy dust I can sprinkle on this situation to get everyone to magically settle down. Our imperfect tools—word, song, chant, ablution, prayer beads, smudge of soot, dab of oil—we use them all, but even the most resourceful chaplain cannot escape the moment when everything in her toolbox fails.

A thin young woman—nose piercing, sweatpants, I have to reduce the cast to the barest of identifying details to keep track—stumbles as if drunk, drapes herself over the body on the bed. An older man tries to remove her.

"NO! LET ME GO! DON'T!"

"Don't act like this. I am going to take you home."

"NO!"

"It won't be finished in a day."

The daughter who is kicking the floor points an accusatory finger at the ceiling.

"I was the STRONG one when she was alive," she shouts. "I FOUGHT for her, I was STRONG for her. SHE GAVE UP ON ME. How could she?!"

This storm will not be stifled. I act on adrenaline, hew to simplicity. Make sure no one gets hurt. Coax saltines and juice boxes into the mouths of those who are close to fainting. Gather everyone for a brief attempt at prayer. Watch the scene fragment back into chaos. Bow to the magnitude and endurance of a maelstrom that shows no sign of abating.

FINALLY, QUIET AS A SPRING breeze, the family's priest glides in with his vestments and scepter. A stately gentleman, beard graying, the ivory of his bejeweled cross bright against black robes. Bible and iPhone in hand, he goes to the head of the bed and begins a liturgy, most of it in Tigre and Ge'ez. He makes no attempt to gather the grieving, just intones on and on, ten minutes, twenty minutes, thirty minutes. He croons to the woman as if singing her to heaven. He sheds tears over her bloodstained face.

It is an hour past midnight when he begins to speak extemporaneously. A family member alerts the priest to my presence. He notices me for the first time, a Chinese face among a sea of Eritrean ones, and grins. "God bless you!"

Instinctively, I join my palms and bow my head. "Thank you for coming, for the honor of listening to the beautiful prayers and songs."

His eyes twinkle. "There is life, and there is death, is there not?"

Later that morning, having barely slept a wink, I walk with K. "You're waking my mind up," she exclaims as we talk about coin-filled dreams. When we arrive back at her star-marked door, I am overcome by exhaustion.

Only then do I raise my rope-burned hand. My supervisor takes one look at me and tells me to go home.

BODHISATTVAS DO RESPOND TO OUR prayers—if we remember we are not beyond help.

Even chaplains forget to pray. Especially for ourselves.

INDEED, THE HOSPITAL WAS FULL of prayers for me.

Every month or so at The Tower, I would meet a fellow Buddhist or writer. Once, even (oh, kindred spirit!) a Buddhist writer. Recently I dreamt of him, though it's been six years since I first walked beneath a string of Tibetan prayer flags to find a white-haired man stooped over a legal pad, scribbling away under the watchful gaze of an enormous thangka. The thangka preceded each of Mr. P's chemo treatments; a family member would hang it up for him before he was wheeled into the room. In my dream, I sensed rather than saw the thangka. Otherwise, the dream wasn't so different from our final visit together.

"Don't give up on the book," he says.

"I won't," I promise.

THE LIBRARIANS OF MY PITTSBURGH childhood would be relieved to know that for all the string-pilfering and call slip–stealing, I loved to read too. The stories in the pages of those library books were as real as our cat's cradle and origami cranes. But, like a bird that refuses to flap even after being folded perfectly, life is not fair. After I am completely nerve-racked by a morning of auditions with other six-year-olds, the local PBS station calls my parents to say they want to cast me. I have already entertained a full-blown fantasy about how this opportunity will banish, once and for all, my compulsive shyness and ungovernable fear, when WQED rescinds the offer, because my parents have told them we are not American citizens, only resident aliens. Life is not fair, because if I am an alien, then I should have supernatural powers like Matilda, and all attempts to move chalk with only my eyes have failed miserably. Life is not fair, because people like me do not get to be on television do not get to be on the spines of books do not get to be household names because ours are unpronounceable and the first thing my day care teachers give me is a way to say my name that Americans won't blanch at and I accept the christening because becoming American is a blanching proposition and the Shanghainese and Mandarin ways of saying my name will never be enough.

So when I promise Mr. P that I won't give up, I am promising what I have long believed to be impossible.

COHERENT NARRATIVES ARE COMFORTING FOR people. Is it to soothe myself or others that I hit upon the formulation "going to Asia to finish a book"? As if going to Asia and finishing a book were somehow related, even though the book is really about America, even though my narrative is threadless, even though there's no coherence. But the formulation is a placating sliver of butter, dulcet and melty on the tongue. It inspires exultant responses. My seatmate on a flight from San Jose to Salt Lake City crows, "You are living the dream!"

What I don't tell him is that it feels more like I am escaping a nightmare.

What I tell myself is that I am lucky. Lucky the psychological violence far outweighed the physical. Lucky that after my stalker comes to the hospital and is awarded a visitor badge for claiming kinship to a female patient whose protected health information he accessed through the database of his government job, the chief of security not only believes me but promises protection whenever I'm on the hospital premises.

I am lucky that the stalking only impels me to move four times during my CPE residency. Lucky no one questions the long hours I spend inside the safety of hospital walls. Lucky I am not the patient whose husband held a cleaver to her neck. Lucky I am not the patient whose boyfriend almost succeeded in running her over with her own car. Lucky I can lose myself in patients' stories and dreams, hopes and fears, what better way to forget my own hauntings, what better way to numb the terror of possible future violence, what better way to stay the humiliation of being admonished by a female Buddhist priest, "you should have known better," as if the news is not festering with the predations of men who should have known better, as if #metoo should be #myfault.

DEAREST FRIEND,

I'm sure you'd have some choice words in response to that "you should have known better." I can hear the low warning growl you reserve for purveyors of callousness and amplifiers of cruelty. Fortunately, before I get a chance to make this about All Of Them (the whole pale-faced black-robed lot), another white female Buddhist priest gives me words to forgive by. "Don't underestimate the trauma," she advises.

Dearest, my biggest regret is how the trauma made me question even our friendship. I regret how my pain prevented me from seeing yours, that incommensurate year of my violation and your father's death. I regret how I didn't drive the eight hours—distance be damned—to see you before boarding that one-way flight to Taiwan. I regret how I convinced myself I didn't have the time, you didn't either or you'd have driven down, which means I made the one assumption all our years of friendship had taught me never to make, the assumption that there'd always be another chance to see you.

Do you still have that wall clock with the jumbled heap of numbers around where four o'clock should be? The clock that otherwise should have been functional, except you hadn't replaced the battery in years? The last time I stayed with you, when we danced the story of our lives in the basement of your parents' home, I wondered about the hour and looked up to see the single word on the clock's face and laughed in utter agreement: "whatever."

After our dance in whatever time, no more sleepovers. Just your father's funeral. And then your hospital room.

You, dear, know my pretend story better than anyone. The truth is, I don't have it together. Dictating suicide letters into the night is no way to envision alternative futures. You understand what it means to see the future as an abyss, but for wholly different reasons. Your early death was encoded in your genes; mine would have been by my own hand.

The patients bless me with a path forward, or should I say backward?* Write that book, they say. Life is short and precious.

---

* *To quote the most bilingual friend I know, a writer and translator of Vietnamese and English poetry:* Projects like these call for many returns, revisions, rereads, cycles of hopes and despair, and lots of waiting, so hahahaha bye forwardness.

Dear friend. Sister spirit. I almost never dream of you. Nor of 奶奶 or 大伯伯, as if some part of me knows: The people you were, while we breathed together on this planet? Those people are gone. Gone altogether beyond.

Dreams are like memories are like those bubbles that delighted me more than anything as a kid, sitting outside the stoop of the laundromat with my dad, blowing delicate iridescent globes from a springy plastic wand, chasing those shimmering shifting surfaces, every so often puncturing them in my nosiness. Skipping toward home, face a film of soapy residue, borne on the benedictory winds of dragony-hot dryer-sheet breath.

"Can you imagine your life without . . . ?" In the safety of my CPE supervisor's presence, I fall apart. I can't, I can't. But in this realm of impermanence, isn't it something we must all do? Prepare for the eventuality—or, more precisely, the inevitability—of losing the ones we love, the ones we can't imagine our lives without.

THE DAY BEFORE SHE DIED, the Eritrean woman said to one of her daughters, "I saw a door open for me."

Relating the story to me, her daughter sighs. "I knew then that she was not long for this world."

DEAR ONE,

I regret I didn't fold a thousand cranes and then more for you.

These sentences I've folded and unfolded and refolded as if our lives depended on it, in the fervent implausible hope that they'll fly your way . . . Will you take these sentences instead?

THE BUTTERFLY NURSE COMES TO me after E dies. "I knew she would fly away from me today. This morning I noticed these little birds on my porch, and I just knew that she would go."

When we first met, E had such perfect posture I asked if she meditated. No, but she had ridden horses all her life. (Same thing, perhaps?)

In our last visit together, E is overheating. The hospital's notoriously cumbersome temperature control system is, as always, taking its sweet time. On a whim, I fold a paper fan, write a blessing on it, and wave its too-flimsy form around her sweating face. E looks abashed to be the center of attention, but also relieved for this paltriest of breezes.

As I fan E, I think of how paper fans—unlike cranes and fortune tellers and a thousand other origami creations—don't require rectangles of paper to be torn into squares. I remember a time in my life when scissors were a luxury, so that one edge of my squares-made-from-rectangles always came out jagged. If my parents could have afforded origami paper, matte colors on one side and shiny silver on the other, would all the cranes of my childhood have flapped? Sometimes, the ones with the rough edges would tear in half before they could move their wings, even though I knew all the folds by heart, even though I would tug the tails that moved the wings with the tenderest insistence.

E and I both came to California by way of the East Coast, though her old home is far enough east that nobody would say *it's really more like the Midwest.* Six years after moving cross-country, on the cusp of becoming a teenager in the Pacific Northwest, I am picking up trash during school-assigned community service day when I find a bird skull among the leaves and litter. Holding that fragment of fleshless bone, I flash back to all those torn birds of my youth, light enough to ride away on the merest breath of wind.

DEAREST,

Long after we have ceremoniously turned off our pagers for the last time at CPE graduation, daaa-daAA-DAAAA! echoes in my dreams, the strident trio of notes haunting my perfectly pitched ears, a cold and broken hallelujah: E flat—B flat—G playing across my pianist's fingertips, the starting black note, the perfect fourth down, the major sixth up to rest on an ivory key.

My dad still dreams of his stint as a university professor thirty years ago, teaching technical English and electronics and Fortran. Each time he wakes up in a cold sweat, sure he's missed class, forgotten his lesson plan, failed to grade the assignments on time.

Like father, like daughter. I wake up in a cold sweat, thinking I'm still in the hospital sleep room, fumbling for my badge, utterly incapable of navigating the labyrinthian path to the people who've paged me. Each time I am beside myself with anxiety: How will I ever be enough?

This is what you will write, in your notebook of little things, while undergoing chemo: "Stay. Here. The mind is masterful at finding fault with the present moment. Life is happening now—enjoy; cry; laugh; yell. When you feel yourself working hard to worry, remember that it is okay to be just where you are and give yourself permission to embrace that."

AS A SPECIAL SPRINGTIME TREAT, a few months before CPE graduation, we get to leave the hospital for a workshop with the intriguing title of "Dreamwork."

Our facilitator V, former director of an AIDS hospice, wears a colorful scarf and sparkling earrings. Her short-cropped hair is streaked with silver. Perched on a stool in her art-filled home, as tabbies prowl the lush garden beyond the French windows, V gives us our first assignment: "Draw a picture of a dream you've had recently, then give your drawing a name."

When it comes time to share, I hold up my crayon sketch and say, "At Death's Door," but everyone mishears it as "At the Store."

Well, that took a turn for the lighthearted.

Q goes last. All we can make out is an indeterminate blob on her sheet of recycled printer paper.

"Tell us more," V urges.

"It's a disc," Q explains. "It's either yellow or brown. Maybe made of light? Shaped like a pothole. Or a sewer cover."

In her dream, Q had stared at the disc, puzzled: *Is this the one? Or is this the one? Which one is the one?*

I am inexplicably seized with giggles. Which *one is the one? Is it important to find the answer? Which* one *is the one? Isn't the question what matters? Which one is the* one?

The rules are that the dreamer speaks first while the rest of us listen. We can present our own perspective on the dream, but its meaning is not for us to interpret.[*]

V asks Q to take on the perspective of the disc.

Time judders to a standstill.

Finally, Q blurts out, "I am . . . the disc!"

Without warning, Q and I begin laughing. I mean, really laughing, busting up laughing, hysterically laughing.

---

[*] Come to think of it, good parameters for chaplaining too

V, looking as mystified as everyone else in the room, wonders if Q-as-the-disc has anything else to say.

"Nothing else," Q responds in between guffaws. "Just, I am . . . I am . . ."

The laughter laughs its way through me. Suddenly I am close to tears.

Seeing the Buddha hold up a flower, Mahakasyapa smiles.

Q is a few years younger than my mother. Despite our differences—generational, racial, religious, cultural—we step to the same soundtrack of worry worry worryworry, our sclerotic dance an agony of second-guessing.

"Sometimes a person will dream a dream for someone else," says V.

Q's dream tells me: Even when we are drowning in doubt—*which one is the one??!*—laughter might just find a way to sneak in.

PART IV: 一路顺风

journey windward

DEAR ONE,

When I arrive in your hospital room, the first thing you say to me is, "Tell me about your world."

I think of this moment eight months later, when I am thirty and you would have been, when a friend of mine who is three years older than us calls me with an update. He too has undergone multiple rounds of chemo and radiation and a transplant, he too has a blood cancer, his too is shaping up to be extremely aggressive. He breaks the news of his grim prognosis, then asks, "Are you ok?"

At your memorial, we will marvel at how much care you bestowed on us. We will shake our heads and say it seems it should have been the other way around. Maybe too there is an undertow of guilt, that in your presence we could feel so good—so loved, so listened to, so embraced—when these cancers and their treatments could only leave their bearers feeling unbearably bad, bad enough to wish for death in order to escape the physical pain alone, to say nothing of the mental and spiritual anguish.

DEAREST,

To get to the hospital to hear you ask about my world, I fly from Phnom Penh to Taipei to San Francisco, spend a restless night in a rented room in a house named for the land of hobbits, step out of the shire's arched front door at sunrise and walk three miles through mossy rain-slicked forest up to your castle in the sky, stop along the way at a plywood sign graffitied over with FUCK CANCER and this rejoinder beneath: Amen.

Your brother tells me that after they built the aerial tram from the waterfront to the hospital, passengers who looked down halfway through the ride would see a giant FUCK THE TRAM banner draped across a rooftop below.

You named the tram Chad.

Later that afternoon, while you nap in your hospital room, your brother and I take Chad—who's only free to ride on the way down, so we plan to jog back up—to the wellness center. At the front desk, the woman looks at me with concern. "You know you have to be eighteen to do yoga here, right?" I'm too embarrassed to tell her that's the age I started doing yoga . . . eleven years ago.*

You named your IV pole—so heavily decorated he put Christmas trees to shame†—Bullwinkle.

As often as possible, despite being tethered, you circumambulate the unit. Your husband lets me do the honors one afternoon. I learn that grabbing Bullwinkle by the scruff is the only way to keep up with your brisk laps. Bullwinkle must be ticklish, because maneuvering him from his belly sends us careening in every direction except the desired one.

This is how you said Amen: "I want to have a cancer party."

---

* I know you have more than your fair share of babyface stories. We the perpetually underaged will exact our revenge in our forties, right?

† Trying to resist a green with envy joke here . . .

GIRL, *YOU THREW THAT PARTY with* style.

For six weeks straight, from the time you left Minnesota and came back to Oregon—turning transplant failure into homecoming celebration—until the wee hours of October 2nd. Guitar was played, hallelujah was sung, cards were made, decorations strung; cakes were eaten, gifts were opened, pedicures given, memories woven.

October 2nd, 3:45 a.m. Your mom will write of your final hours: the love in the room was palpable, to say we are heartbroken does not begin to capture the excruciating sense of loss.

We forgot that the absence of fresh flowers meant someone was immunocompromised here. Surely not the beauty who is making a music video in her Turnip-the-Beet shirt, rocking a half-shaved head while belting out "Bad Blood"* over Taylor Swift's soprano.

---

* *Has your sense of humor always been this wicked?*

Dearest one,

I ask what has surprised you the most.

The love, you say, the outpouring of love, how much of it there has been, unremitting. The fiancé-quickly-turned-husband's devotion.

Of course, the relapse too. That wasn't such a happy surprise.

Thank you for loving us all so much, I say. And for letting us love you.

I wish this conversation could last forever. I know you need to rest. We hug, gingerly. My whole body tingles. Next time, hugs will be verboten. You are afraid there won't be a next time. Somehow I know there will be. I have the flight booked already, less than a month from now.

I don't want that next time to be the last . . . but it will be. The last time.

THAT OUTPOURING OF LOVE AT the end is never guaranteed.

During my first visit with Mr. X, we discover our fathers are both from Shanghai. From his hospital room, we watch the afternoon sun peep through a copse of trees, dappling the spire of the church across the way. Mr. X tells me about his Catholic parents. He smiles remembering how he never wanted to go to Sunday service as a kid, would only trudge along for the free lunch afterward.

"There are so many things we don't know when we're young," Mr. X sighs.

Later he lived in Hong Kong. He came to America for the sake of his daughter.

And then? 困难, 痛苦, 失去. Decades hardened into difficulty, pain, loss.

"This is the lot of first-generation immigrants," Mr. X sighs.

And then: steely silence. Just as I am getting a window into his life, the hurricane shutters come crashing down. His hardship, his suffering, his losses—Mr. X will bear them to the grave.

It is not my job to pry. And yet . . .

Sometimes, cultural familiarity is not an asset. I am keenly aware that his daughter is my age, and that she is not visiting. I hear my mom's warning refrain: let sleeping dogs lie. Mute the past. Muzzle history. I am keenly aware that we do not talk with our Chinese elders about the likelihood that they will die soon. Who is protecting whom? Arriving in Shanghai at the age of eighteen during my gap year, I am shocked to see my favorite uncle's ravaged body. No one had told me he was dying.

"If it's my time to go, then there's nothing I can do; these bodies don't last forever," Mr. X sighs. Is this pragmatism or despair? He wants to read the Chinese newspaper but refuses my offer to pick one up for him. Is this politeness (don't want to be a burden) or hopelessness (nothing matters anymore)?

MY MOTHER IS A DAUGHTER of the Chinese Cultural Revolution. She is also a daughter of the man I called 外公, whose two-character name I gleaned for a middle school family tree project, only to learn years later that it was not his real name at all.

The second character of my Waigong's pseudonym is homophonous with the second character of the street I called home for the first four and a half years of my life. I had thought the street I lived on was named after mountain shade while my grandfather was named after leafy secrets. Three decades after leaving Shanghai, I realize it's the exact opposite. The truth is mountain secrets, leafy shade.

My mother's unknowables are also my own. Like the first American game show that graced the grainy fifteen-inch screen of our first American TV, we can only end on questions. What is Waigong's name before he changed it to the one recorded in our family tree? What is the cause of my mother's half-brother's death during the CCR, and if murder, at whose hands? What is muted past, muzzled history?

CULTURAL HABIT STIFLES MY VISITS with Mr. X. I can't bring myself to ask, as I do with non-Chinese patients, "Would you like me to visit again?" A question so direct would be kryptonite to his superblanket of secure, smothering secrecy.

When I knock, Mr. X always says come in. I wonder if he is disappointed that I am not his elusive doctor. Days become weeks become more than a month. I visit periodically. Mr. X is always wearing a hospital-issue gown, the chicken-poxed-frog effect ghastly against his worsening pallor.

One afternoon, I see a visitor hurrying out of his room. Intercepting her, I introduce myself in Chinese. She asks if Mr. X is depressed, then apologizes for rushing off. When I mention to Mr. X that I spoke to his girlfriend (as she introduced herself), he says she's just a neighbor. I comment on the pink flowers she brought, the only spot of color in a room devoid of personal effects. He shrugs. The Chinese newspapers I gave him have disappeared.

Time is suspended in Mr. X's room. His plan of care is uncertain. There are rumors that his doctor—who has a reputation for prescribing aggressive treatments and avoiding bedside encounters—wants to operate, but even I know that someone with cachexia this severe could never survive surgery.

Another time I meet a man whose self-proclaimed status (neighbor) is undisputed by Mr. X. This friend hopes the surgery will 改善 the situation. But the word that comes to mind when I think of Mr. X is 等死.

What does it mean to make things better when you are waiting for death?

STRAINED BEDFELLOWS, IMPROVEMENT AND DYING. On the cusp of Chinese New Year, I wonder aloud if his daughter will come. Mr. X shrugs: forget about her. Same response when I ask after his neighbors: 不要管他们.

没办法. Nothing to be done.

He becomes skeletal. How swift the body's mutiny, how assured its disobedience and decline. One day he can't even take a sip of water unassisted. Another day he is shivering uncontrollably. I ask at the nursing station to have the room heated up. In a cheap motel room you can crank up a plastic dial and hear clanging evidence of the temperature rising. But heating this hospital room involves the charge nurse calling another department that presumably fiddles with some black box to make an invisible vent start emitting warmer air.

I can't tell if the room is warming up. Is the nurse on hold? Did the climate control department get the right room? Is the patient next door sweltering? Does the placebo effect apply in this situation: Is it just that we need to believe it's working? But Mr. X's teeth are still chattering.

I bring him heated water, which involves taking cold water and microwaving it in a flimsy paper cup. I wish there was a hot water dispenser, like in every Chinese household I've ever been to. But in the storage room to which my badge grants special access, there are only cold things, ice and ice water and Jell-O, a sad and frigid pantry. I want to give Mr. X the 热水袋 of my childhood, that voluptuous chocolate-brown mass with its elegantly tapered neck, lurking beneath the heavy blankets at the foot of my bed, radiating warmth and ready to undulate at the slightest touch of a toe. Homely jiggling evidence that Mama or Baba or Nainai love me enough to wrestle this unwieldy beast into slumbering submission.

DURING CPE ORIENTATION, WE'RE TAUGHT to chart every chaplaincy visit, even the uneventful ones. More frequently now, my notes say *Attempted Visit: Mr. X was asleep, will follow-up*. I do not write that my heart aches to see the sunken eyes in his jaundiced face.

A woman on the same unit has the same metastatic cancer diagnosis. We use the interpreter phone to converse, since she only speaks Vietnamese. She is eager for her son to come from the East Coast, a visit our social worker is arranging.

On my eighth visit with Mr. X, we have talked for a few minutes when a stricken expression crosses his face. I notice a wet spot blooming at the waist of his hospital gown and panic—there's no time to call his nurse. He gestures urgently toward the plastic urinal. I grab it. He's too weak to pry off the lid. I yank off the cap. Mr. X moans in pain, 哎呀, 哎呀. I avert my eyes. Another plastic urinal hangs morosely from the edge of his hospital bed like a broken-necked 热水袋.

不好意思, he apologizes afterward, his voice a raspy whisper. No, no, I protest, blinking back tears. 没什么, 不要紧, it's nothing, 你现在身体弱, 应该有人帮你, your body is weak right now, there should be people here to help you.

TEN YEARS AGO TO THE month, in January 2005, the man who is dying is my uncle. This is not possible; he is invincible. I knew vaguely of his treatments. I did not know they could only stave and not cure. I did not yet know that if you had to play the morbid game of pick-a-cancer, his would not be a good choice. As a chaplain resident, I will glean the bad ones from the oncology nurses and doctors, who betray them through a constriction of their faces, a tightening of their voices, an avoidance of the topic of prognosis—death ultimately calling their bluff.

My uncle never smoked, but his father, my 爷爷, did. Yeye died of emphysema. In April 1992, one year after I board my first plane, Yeye can't find a cab to take him to a family reunion and decides to bike there. He makes it to the venue, just barely, but never recovers from the ill-advised attempt. On a bookshelf in my parents' California home is a photo of Nainai holding my dad: a chubby two-year-old clutches his father's pipe, the bowl trapped inside his clasped hands, the bit between his pouting lips. In my mind the image has a phantom twin: my grandfather gasping by the side of the road next to his collapsed bicycle, 四川北路 long behind him, his oldest sister's house in 卢湾区 close by. But of course that second image was never birthed from the vinegary bath of the makeshift home darkroom where my parents developed their black-and-white photos.

Only in my early thirties will I find out that my father left China knowing he would never see his father again, would not be there for Yeye's death, would not have the money or the right visa to go back for the funeral.

困难, 痛苦, 失去. Is this the lot of first-generation immigrants? Does this explain why my earliest memory is serrated with dread? We are leaving Shanghai and the grown-ups I love are avoiding my question of when I will see them again. 明天? 后天? I can think of life only in 天s, seven of which make up a 星期, uncountable many of which go into 月s and 年s, those unfathomable caverns of yawning time. When I raise my voice to demand an answer, the grown-ups say "soon, soon," and the bald-faced lie of it makes me scream harder—when? WHEN?! TELL ME WHEN!

THIS IS HOW, AT THE age of four, I am ripped away from all that I know and love.

I can count on one hand the number of times I see my uncle again after that day. He never stops being a whole world to me. His hugs tell me 回家了. Without them I am 无家可归, no home to return to.

In January 2005, I call my uncle's only brother. *Dad,* I say through gritted teeth. *Come back.* My father asks if he can wait a week. *No. Get the emergency visa. COME BACK NOW.*

This time, he makes it for the death and the funeral.

OUR SOCIAL WORKER HAS FINALLY tracked down Mr. X's daughter, who lives a long plane ride away. She calls to inform her that her father is dying. The daughter is resolute: Don't call me again. I worked hard to cut off all contact. And no, I don't want to know when he dies.

WHAT MEMORIES RICOCHET IN MR. X's mind, in this silent room with the fading flowers and decamping newspapers? Chaplains aren't mind readers. Some things we will never know. Some things we will only sense, in the weight of the unspoken, in the stale air of a room that may or may not be warming up.

THE FOLLOWING MONDAY, I SCAN the patient list before oncology morning rounds. There is a new name attached to the room across from the Catholic church. The charge nurse confirms that Mr. X died in the night.

He had said, 你已经帮了我很多了, though it's hard not to wish I could have done more.

Now, to my desire to help, I can only say: 没办法, nothing to be done. And also: Who is helping whom?

Early on in his hospitalization, Mr. X was terrified he would lose his Section 8 housing in Chinatown because he couldn't leave the hospital for a routine inspection of his apartment. Thanks to our social worker's deft orchestrations, the crisis passed. The inspection was delayed. Mr. X slumped with relief.

He would never return to that apartment. But some part of me feels I will find him there, sipping coffee in the mornings, reading the Chinese newspaper, heading out for a leisurely walk around his neighborhood. Some part of me needs to know that his hard life once held these small comforts, he who had lost so much else.

DEAR ONE,

The day my 奶奶 dies, I write a three-thousand-word essay.* Four years later, I read it aloud to you. It is like reading a eulogy at the funeral she never had. I'd forgotten the essay existed, had no memory of ever writing it. Cleaning up one's computer files should not be undertaken lightly.

Nainai's was a life without spiritual preferences. As you know, that didn't stop her roommates at the rehab center from praying for her.

My favorite is the Filipina grandmother who scoots on over to our side of the room during the hospice nurse's visits. She maneuvers over to us by pedaling fuzzy sock–clad feet against the linoleum, urine bag swaying precariously close to her wheelchair's spokes.† Her aide scolds her in a mix of exasperated English and Tagalog. "Nanay! You are not supposed to get up. This your bed, not that one!" Undeterred, she sidles up to my nainai and starts praying. Guaranteed effective prayers, she announces with pride—not for nothing is she the mother of a Catholic priest who served in Papua New Guinea.** The hospice nurse asks if my grandmother is Catholic. I shake my head no. Dismayed, the nurse hastens to dissuade our eager interloper. "She is not Catholic, ma'am, so please keep your prayers to yourself . . . or . . . um . . . pray for the world! Yes, the world! Pray for world peace!"

Or maybe my favorite is the Mexican grandmother swathed in a fleece tiger blanket, the feline's four-foot-wide head flashing beneath a light-up necklace of chili pepper–shaped Christmas bulbs. The abuela speaks to herself in a steady stream of Spanish, but I think she knows this rehab center has become nursing home and now hospice for my grandmother. I glimpse the tears at the corners of her eyes when she looks at Nainai, the way she lets Nainai prop her feet against her tiger-wrapped legs when they sit together at the cafeteria. Where's the benediction in this, my mom's coworker would surely ask, but I know I don't need to explain it to you.

---

* *Don't worry, I won't rehash it here.*

† *Well, I won't rehash all of it here.*

** *Ok, indulge me retelling some of it here . . .*

Of course if I have to pick favorites I'd choose my own grandmother, even on the day she tears off her oxygen tube and refuses to eat. When the winsome male nurse tries to feed her, Nainai lets the spooned morsel sit in her mouth for a heart-stopping second before spitting it onto her bib. Then, with wordless fury, she hurls the blob of canned peach to the ground with an arm we thought had gone limp.

She refuses to eat and I refuse to leave, even after she finds her voice and calls me by my pet name, demanding 不要管我, 不要管我, 不要管我 *with increasing intensity. Soon she's hollering her demands:* leave me be, never mind me, forget about me. *But I can't leave, can't never mind, can't forget. Finally her voice modulates to a guttural and shaky chant,* 放心, 放心, 放心, fangxin, *don't worry, let go the heart. The response I can't utter is* 捨不得, 捨不得, 捨不得, how unbearable it is to part.

The daughter of another Chinese grandma at the rehab center overhears Nainai's chant. "We can all fangxin *once you start eating and get better and go home," she chirps. I am simultaneously touched by her concern and offended by her saccharine promise. Who is she shitting? Nainai and I both know she will die soon. We let that spurious bait—do X and Y is assured—go the way of the canned peach.*

That night they put my grandmother on antidepressants. Tubes and IVs inserted during two emergency room visits will follow. In the end, morphine.

I hear the garage door open at 3 a.m., my dad home from his vigil. Two hours later, the call. When we go to pick up her scant belongings, the hospice nurse addresses us in the third person and mistakes Nainai for a grandfather. "How is the family coping with his passing?" I look around for the phantom people she's inquiring after. "The family did not want a feeding tube," the hospice nurse informs us. I start to explain, then notice her tight-lipped frown.

We arrange for a witness cremation. My dad struggles with the word, asks if I want to attend the witness cri-mi-na-tion. Who is accusing whom?

The family does not allow me at the bedside for my grandmother's death, just as they do not allow me at the bedside for the death of her oldest son, my favorite uncle. Who is protecting whom?

This isn't much of a eulogy, is it?

Nainai had two sons, ten years apart, the second at the request of the first. As young men in their respective homes—on a street named for mountain secrets, on a street named for a faraway western province—each would put curtains on the windows of a small room from which they would birth images of their daughters from a vinegary bath.

Really more threnody than eulogy.

The recycling bin eats a raft of white-capped orange bottles. Atenolol and methimazole and propranolol and warfarin and more, a sad and frightening pantheon. The nailbed of my left thumb is bleeding from punching pills out of their packaging into the trash can. Silver carcasses of spent blister packs drift on a sea of pink and white and gray and mustard yellow capsules. My grandmother was not religious, but she clearly believed in medicine.

In the last of the two emergency room visits, I remark that Nainai has a strong grip. "She's just strong, period," the attending nurse exclaims.

I miss those strong arms that thrust bamboo poles from her balcony perch with the precision of a javelin thrower, poles twice my height from which our laundry danced. Those strong arms to which I clung as we walked from her Shanghai apartment to the 小菜场 to fetch the day's fresh veggies and a handful of pork bones. Those strong arms that enveloped me in a final embrace, my head against her chest, the rasp of fluid-filled lungs, she old and I grown, but like always it was I who needed the holding more than she.

In Nainai's letters to me on onionskin paper, the third and final paragraph is always about her flowers. Her new apartment has no backyard, the flowers don't do as well on the sill, but 没办法, it can't be helped. The letter's opening line is always the same—when Nainai is gone, who will call me by my pet name? One letter informs me of the pork bone soup that is the favorite Nainai-made food of the tangle of gray that is my cousin's (so, Nainai's) newly adopted dog. The first paragraph always ends with three words. 我爱你. When I find these letters again, a quarter century after they were written, I have to hold them at arm's length. Otherwise I'd ruin them with my blubbering.

The bereavement booklet that I've tucked in a folder with Nainai's death certificate suggests a two-month window for grief's capricious sojourn. Reading this a decade later, I laugh and laugh and laugh. I think you, dear friend, would too.

As a chaplain volunteer at the as-real-as-it-gets community hospital, I enter into my first family meeting. It's a tense tableau.

The family members stand, arms crossed and stony-faced, next to the medical interpreter.

The man whose fate is being discussed cannot join the conversation. Sixty-six days ago, he had a heart attack while out jogging and wasn't found for over an hour. Now his options are being measured in a cramped, windowless room. We hear a cascade of creaks and groans every time the upstairs toilet flushes.

The doctor wants a Cantonese-speaking Buddhist. I do not speak Cantonese, I am not yet comfortable identifying as Buddhist, but the bigger point is, demographics are not determinative. People are messy, people confound categories, categories quail at all this variation. Even if I speak their dialect (which I don't) and share their religion (they've given no indication of being Buddhist), what right do I have to coerce them into acting as the doctor deems fit?

The doctor is on a roll. "His brain shows no signs of improvement." Diagrams, images, statistics. "He cannot make a meaningful recovery." Diagrams, images, statistics. "He is not capable of intelligent action." "He cannot think." (Are these the same thing?) Diagrams, images, statistics. "He's not the dad or brother you knew, he'll never be like that again." The interpreter can barely keep up with the torrent of words.

I empathize with the doctor's desire to put a do-not-resuscitate order in place. Without the DNR, if the patient suffers another cardiac arrest, the outcome will likely be the same—death—but with more broken ribs. How frightening it must be for the nurses too, to believe this man can only worsen under their care. They are thinking of bedsores, aspiration pneumonia, iatrogenic illnesses.

But the family insists: It's only been sixty-six days. He needs more time. He is improving. We massage his limbs every day. I feel his arms getting stronger. He still looks like my dad. When he looks at me, it's as if he's really looking at me, only he can't talk anymore. So I don't know, what you're telling me, that he can't see me or hear me—I just don't know.

They are not swayed by logos (the statistics, the charts), nor by ethos (these resources could be used for someone who *can* make a "meaningful recovery"). The doctor tries pathos. "My own father was in a similar situation. I think we caused a lot of suffering. And now I wish we hadn't done all those things." Unimpressed by this confession, the family remains stony-faced, arms pretzeled even tighter than an hour ago.

The meeting ends inconclusively. Later I see the family uncap a bottle of greenish liquid and commence with a vigorous massage of the bedbound figure as they speak to him in Toishanese. We exchange a few words in Mandarin, but mostly they ignore me.

Seventy-three days after the heart attack, he's still there, in the same room with another Chinese man of the same age. The new arrival has had a stroke, the doctors are pessimistic about the prognosis, and the family has asked to keep him on life support for a bit longer as they think things over.

To the passive figure in the bed, I say a few words in English before switching to Mandarin, though I'm not sure if this is his dialect. No response. I rise to leave, pretending I have somewhere else to be, when really it's my own discomfort driving me out of the room.

That's when I notice the tears in his eyes.

In the end, I stayed an hour, holding the man's hand, speaking occasionally. He heaves with sobs when I say 中國, that middle kingdom that was once his home. When I wipe the mucus from his face he only cries harder. Before he withdraws back into his original state of immobility, he moves his right hand to grab mine with a firm squeeze. He never uttered a word.

This is the moment—my four grandparents' and favorite uncle's deaths behind me, a best friend's death ahead of me—that I capitulate. Chaplaincy can't be what I do in the interstices of three part-time jobs. Someday I will need to surrender myself to the yearlong, full-time training.

MY DEAR,

You'll visit many a hospital in your life, but not the one where I did my year-long CPE training. Like the hospital where you will spend your final days, this one employs a massage therapist. I can leave N a message anytime, ask her to visit so-and-so in room #### when she's at The Tower next. Ours is a natural alliance, since she prioritizes working with cancer patients and I've remained on oncology through the fall and spring semesters, will be staying on through the shorter summer semester too.

N says I have a calm beyond my years. I want to demur, but I thank her because I am learning to accept compliments.

Another woman I love to run into is the phlebotomist. "Girrrrl!" she exclaims the first time we meet. "How'd you get those biceps?" Look who's talking, I rib. "Crossfit!" she grins proudly. Once upon a time I swam and did yoga several days a week, but in this sleep-deprived year I'm lucky to squeeze in a weekly jog. So, in answer to her question, what my mama gave me?

The phlebotomist lets out a low whistle when she glimpses my badge. "I could never do your job," she declares. There's no way I could do hers either. The very suggestion of a needle makes me woozy. The sight of blood threatens to have me on a gurney in two seconds flat. I probably should have thought of these things before I signed up to work in a hospital.

"Focus on your gifts, not your lack," my supervisor urges.

When we pass each other in the hospital halls, the phlebotomist and I curl our biceps and give each other a snappy high five.

I think you'd approve, dear friend. I believe you called this the purpose of these human lives: loving on each other like nobody's business.

"OH, JUST WHO I WAS looking for!" It's a warm day in late spring and N is on the oncology unit for a massage request. She's just come from the outpatient clinic, where a delightful older woman struck up a conversation and started reminiscing about a chaplaincy visit from last fall. The patient had forgotten the chaplain's name, but it was a young Asian woman (so, me). I try to place the patient; there have been hundreds since then. N gives me some more details, and it clicks. Oh, yes! I've forgotten her name too, but not our visit. I wish I could teleport to the clinic this instant, catch her before she leaves, ask if her beloved parakeet is still ok.

WHEN PATIENTS GET DISCHARGED FROM the hospital, I offer blessings, thinking of my nainai, who would say to me before every trip, 一路顺风.

That windward benediction cloaked me in safety and soundness, anytime and everywhere. The words apotropaic, like the designated pair of chopsticks in Nainai's kitchen that were mine alone, not just for that meal but for always. Like the tapered glass bottle delivered in the predawn just for me, its contents emptied into a bowl and served piping hot, the milky beginning to my every Shanghai breakfast. Like the saucer of freshly made pork bone soup especially for 贝贝, the shaggy mop of a dog my grandma doted on. Like Nainai's strong arms that gathered bamboo poles laden with laundry from her balcony perch, poles twice my height and never a single sock lost.

When Chinese patients leave the hospital, I wish them 保重 or 走好 or 一路顺风, then let slip a 再见 as I wave goodbye. It's not that I hope we'll meet again inside these hospital walls, but *zaijian* is a farewell so ubiquitous I forget its literal meaning of *let's meet again*.

OUR JEWISH CHAPLAIN RELAYS THE news that another patient remembers me.

Even though it's after 5 p.m., even though my next twenty-four-hour on-call shift is in two days, I rush over.

Zaijian has come true. Mama J greets me with a smile; I can see that even this takes enormous effort. Her breathing is labored. "Please, Mama, save your energy, rest," her daughter and I beg. But she insists on saying a few words anyway. 你還好嗎?

I assure her I'm well, although the truth is I'm burning out.

She asks after the boy who is going to Cambodia. Will I join him there after the program is finished? I confess I'm not sure, that I've been thinking of going to Taiwan.

It's past your work hours, she reminds me. You should go home and eat dinner.

We are supposed to say to patients that we will *try* to visit, just in case something comes up, so that we don't inadvertently break our promises. But I can't figure out how to say this in Chinese, the *try* an interloper in an otherwise simple sentence, so I promise I will visit her tomorrow.

Friday is a busy day. Again it's after 5 p.m. before I'm able to stop by. Again she shoos me home to eat and rest, ignoring my protestations that it's no trouble at all for me to stay awhile.

Outside the hospital room, I listen to her daughter's account of how mom ended up back in the hospital. *She was twice at death's door, but recovered each time, came home with us.* 不久以前她還好好的! *But then . . .* There is a quaver of fear beneath the fierceness in her voice.

In two years I will think the exact same thing. She was *just fine* when we Skyped last month, she did everything right, *how could this happen*—and I will want something to blame and I will be seething and then I will find myself sobbing on the floor, crushed by the weight of not knowing how many days would remain.

ONE DAY. ONE DAY WOULD remain for Mama J.

Like the other residents, I've had a twenty-four-hour on-call shift every week for the past eight months. Weekdays, we can refer to our colleagues; weekends, the on-call chaplain flies solo. This is the busiest on-call shift I've had yet. My pager has been beeping nonstop. The requests come from all three hospital campuses—as soon as I've finished one visit, I'm rushing off to the next.

daaa-daAA-DAAAA! It's R, one of the social workers on oncology.

"Mrs. J is dying. Can you come?"

"Yes of course, I'm at the other campus, but I'll drive over now."

I trip down the stairs to the parking lot, tremble as I start the car, curse my carelessness as I hit a curb on the way out, try not to speed down the familiar three-mile drag.

And how it drags. Every intersection is red, the traffic lights channeling a familiar refrain from our supervisors: death is not an emergency.

THE DOOR IS AJAR; HER nurse ushers me in. The atmosphere is subdued. Mama J is no longer speaking. I say hello to her daughter, introduce myself to her son who has just arrived from a flight across the Pacific.

"Can she hear us?" he asks.

"We can't know for sure, but people often say hearing is the last sense to go," I reply.

I model what I mean. *J* 媽媽 . . .

Leaning close to her ear, resting my hand lightly on hers, voice wobbly and eyes prickling, I speak to her in our mutual language of Mandarin. *Your children are here by your side, 放心, don't worry. I am grateful for our conversations. You have taught me so much about being kind to others. I'm moved by how much you love and care for your children and grandchildren. And here is your capable nurse, V, she says she's giving you just a small dose of medicine to help you relax because your blood pressure looks a bit high. 放心, don't worry, it shouldn't hurt because it's going directly into your IV.*

I repeat 放心, let go the heart. But really I am 捨不得, hating to part.

I leave Mama J with her children sitting on either side, daughter grasping her right hand, son holding her left. I have another visit to go to, but I tell them to page me at any point if they want me to come back.

THEY PAGE AGAIN A COUPLE hours later. Mama J has just breathed her last.

Her daughter tells me mom's last words were 謝謝. Thank you.

What are the causes and conditions that made it possible . . .

I don't know. But I am grateful.

"Unfortunate," the doctor declares. After surviving the surgery and recovering from near-paralysis well enough to start cooking for her grandchildren again, the metastasis.

"Unlucky," Mama J had sighed one quiet afternoon during her first hospitalization. "But I don't feel sorry for myself. I feel very lucky to have had all this time with my grandchildren."

Now her daughter looks stunned. "她二十分鐘前走了." It's been twenty minutes since her mom died. 走了, walked away, in the parlance of our shared mother tongue.

"你想她現在在哪裡?" I can see the question has been tormenting her.

I hesitate a moment. "I don't know where she is now. . . . Where do you feel she is?"

"我們沒有信仰. 佛教有甚麼想法呢?" I knew from Mama J that their family didn't subscribe to a faith, but I am surprised by her daughter's second question: What's the Buddhist perspective?

Now is not the time for a sermon. I offer the simplest response I can think of. "Different Buddhists believe in different things. Some believe in rebirth."

She shakes her head no. "I don't want her to be reborn! I want her to stay with us at home forever and watch over us."

I feel a lump in my throat.

She continues: "There are people who say we become buddhas . . ."

I nod. "Yes, some Buddhists believe when our loved ones die they become buddhas or bodhisattvas, never to suffer again, accompanying us always."

Mama J's daughter starts ruminating on what could have been. Hawaii. Grandma at the kids' high school graduations, their weddings—"The kids! How will I tell them?? They're so young."

Deep breath. "I know it's tempting to shield them from the truth, but I bet they already intuit—"

"Yes, I think they know their grandma has . . ."

Her voice cracks.

THAT NIGHT THE PAGER FALLS SILENT—

finally, I cry myself

into an exhausted, dreamless sleep.

Awakened by a crystalline clarity,

a poignant peace,

I find myself smiling.

謝謝, I say.

一路顺风

PART V: 不远千里

distance no matter

DEAREST YOU,

I don't remember whose whim it was, T's or mine, to grab veggie burgers at the retro diner. Usually we opt for the vegan Japanese place I brought you to the last time you were in town, or the Ethiopian and Burmese restaurants you'll have to try on your next visit. Anyway, we're about to walk into the flamingo-pink interior when I spot someone I know at one of the white vinyl booths.

Mama J's daughter is sitting there with her husband and kids.

I'm about to rush through the double doors to say hello when I catch myself. It's normal to get attached to families you've spent a lot of time with at the hospital. "But," our supervisors caution, "before you make yet another unsolicited visit, ask yourself: 'Whose need?'"

"Let's come back another time," I say to T, keeping mum about my reasons.

UNBEKNOWNST TO THE FAMILY, NURSE B fought for Mama J not to be put in a body bag.

B is unrelenting with the men from the mortuary. "It's only a few steps, you can cover her with a simple white sheet!" she protests. The men don't know that B's mother died in the Philippines a year ago, how awful it was to see her taken away like a sack of potatoes. Two years later I will see B's ferocity in sculpture form, on the bulging face of a twelfth-century Ungyo at the south gate of Todaiji in a city of roving sika deer.

Mama J glides away shrouded in white cotton, spared the indignity of being stuffed in black plastic. I help her children pack up her belongings. They had clearly become acquainted with the hospital's temperamental climate control system: a floor fan towers above various odds and ends.

Her reticent son comments that he can't place my Chinese accent.

Her daughter laments, *I had such hopes. I wanted to take her to Hawaii . . . and mama loved Europe . . .*

DEAR LOVE,

I had such hopes, too.

Hawaii, New Zealand, Santorini, Ireland . . .

Especially Ireland. Especially after that one-unit class where our quirky lec-
turer—psychotherapist, pizza-lover, erstwhile marathon runner[*]—regaled us
with stories[†] and non sequiturs.[**]

You teased me for reading the Bulletin cover to cover at the start of every quarter, perusing even the courses I was not remotely qualified for, in departments we
never dreamed existed. Behold this tasty morsel: "Principles and Practices for the
Care of the Dying."

All five of us were late the first day because we couldn't find the portable where
the class was being held, way beyond the med school near the shopping center. Of
the many people we stopped to ask, not one had heard of the room, the class, or
the professor. We were convinced it was all a figment of our imaginations when—
voilà! Into the rabbit hole we fell.

The class was me and you and the Buddhist boyfriend and another undergrad
I'd somehow convinced to join us and someone else who has since faded from
memory—what was her name?

It was like no class we had ever taken: Nary an assignment. More fable than
lecture. Our Irish professor's stories a thicket of illogicality. We couldn't decipher
the half of it. We laughed so hard we nearly cried and vowed to go someday to the
land that could produce someone so deliciously whimsical.

---

[*] Did you ever make heads or tails of how the marathon running was related to his emigrating
from Ireland to the US at the age of eighteen, long before we were born?

[†] E.g., the wake where the dead man was too big to fit through the front door, so they used a
window

[**] On bringing pizza to class: "I'll give you a dollar!"

A LITTLE THAI BOY IS punching me in Bangkok. Why has he singled me out, here at this international Buddhist women's conference, as nuns eat roti by the lotus pond during a break between panel presentations? I don't speak his language, so I can't ask.

I let this five-year-old stranger pummel me. No mom or auntie or nanny comes to claim him. His fists are too small to hurt, though each strike surprises me. I wonder if I should yell at him to stop—will he hit other women in the future?—but then I worry it will look like I am the one trying to hurt him. What if I have hurt him, in a previous lifetime?

It is the summer three years before my CPE residency. I have just come from another conference where T, not yet a PhD student, was unexpectedly invited to present his research after a professor had to drop out. It is our first time in Taiwan. We fall in love with it, Jinshan Jiufen Keelong Hualien Kaohsiung Taipei whose spellings scramble my pinyin-accustomed eye, friendly people colorful temples vegetarian buffets tropical fruit everywhere we go.

At the Buddhist studies conference in Taiwan, the presentations are over my head—full of Sanskrit and Pali, Sogdian and Manchu, how these scholars learn all the languages required for this field is beyond me—but I am enamored of the venue, a Buddhist monastery-college on a mountain in a rural area abutting the sea. The food is tasty and vegan. The monastics are studious and kind. The campus is peaceful and immaculate. How wonderful it would be to come back here for longer than six days, I muse. A few weeks perhaps, maybe even a few months.

Wishes made in monasteries should not be undertaken lightly.

FOUR YEARS LATER, IN THE class where our beloved woodcarving professor asks how it is that we all came to be here, I meet a filmmaker-translator-writer who studied philosophy in college and whose sister is working in America as a music therapist. Other students talk about this talented young Taiwanese woman in hushed tones of admiration. Forgoing a slew of more prestigious opportunities, she has opted to study on the mountain with us for this year.

She tells us she is here to 還願. She does not tell us how it came to be that she made this vow that brings her to us. But in that simple word, *huanyuan,* there is an answer to our teacher's question.

We could not be here without debts of gratitude.

IS THERE A DANGER TO this translation, which invokes a debt whose depth, one suspects, is bottomless? 願 is *hope, wish, desire, vow* (made before a Buddha, say), 願 is *honest* and *ready*. 還 is *still, yet, in addition,* but in its other pronunciation, the correct one for 還願, it is *return* as in *to native home* & *giving back* as in *the library books* & *repayment* as in *the money lent* & *retribution* as in *eye for an eye*. Revenge exacted in kind, how strange that we use the word *kind* for this elocution.

I find the Buddhist teaching that everyone was once your mother at once breathtaking and unsettling. Because there are all kinds of mothers. Because mothers, like all people, are capable of love and protection—and their opposites. If a mother says to her child, I wish you'd never been born, the child is annihilated. If a child says to her mother, I wish you'd never been born, she annihilates both of them. If your aunt says that you and your mother 没有母女缘, do you rest in the relief of untethering, or do you snag on the oxymoron that you can't, by dint of biological fact, not have mother-daughter affinity?

After encountering the Buddhist text on how it is children who choose their parents and not vice versa, I never again shout at my mother that I didn't ask to be born. When I think I'd rather be a deva or demigod or demon or dugong—anything to wriggle out of the skin I'm in—there's that pesky how-rare-this-human-rebirth business to contend with.

Sleeping dogs lie. Muzzled pasts mute. You never recoup the losses, you learn to live with them. When it comes to metaphors of debt, I can only end on questions. What do we owe our parents? Everything? Nothing? What do we owe each other? Anything? Everything?

DEAR ONE,

T and I were at the bookstore near our favorite Indian restaurant in Phnom Penh today. There was this young Cambodian boy in the stationery section poking people's bottoms, which were at face level for him. Specifically, he was poking the derrieres of attractive women. His mother scolded him in Khmer, and then, reaching her wits' end, hollered at him in English, "Don't touch people's butts!"

—

Walking up the cobweb- and cockroach-encrusted stairwell of our apartment complex, we are greeted by squawking from the floor above. Lok Yeay (who feeds the cats and talks casually of the inevitability of her death) tells us our upstairs neighbors have purchased an exorbitantly expensive parrot. It's an investment: if they can just train it to speak Khmer, it will be worth even more than what they paid for it, something in the magnitude of hundreds of dollars. Months later, the parrot vocalese continues to sound like SQUAWK to me and not ជំរាបសួរ and សុខសប្បាយទេ, but to be fair my Cambodian has become no more intelligible either.

—

Every morning when I jog along the Tonle Sap, on the stretch before it joins the Mekong, I pass by the bird-sellers. The cages, no taller than my waist, are crammed with brown sparrows that twitter and flutter in a chaos of feathers and birdseed. It's the hot dry season and the cracked sidewalks are caked with the poop of the sparrows' unfettered cousins, the fat pigeons that eat the kernels (sold by the popcorn-sellers) thrown to them by toddlers (three-quarters of the people in this country are younger than I am, how's that for feeling over the hill at thirty?)—who sometimes chase the winged gray rats (as my dad would call them) into a cloud of flapping and cooing (which is cute until one of the flying rodents hits me in the face). It's an ingenious business model: people pay for the karmically propitious act of releasing a sparrow, the sparrows always come back for the birdseed. I've resigned myself to jogging on sticky sidewalk, but I do try to avoid stepping on the dead sparrows, splayed and spent and free at last from their job of merit-making for the people.

—

On my morning jogs I often see a red-collared golden retriever who strains against his matching red leash with so much excitement I expect the tether to snap at any minute. It's as if every day every thing is BRAND NEW (squirrel!). Can we distill this special brand of doggedly amnestic appreciation and imbibe it with our daily multivitamins? After the umpteenth time of passing each other on this pungent street (which, rather unbelievably, was known as the Champs-Élysées of Phnom Penh a century ago), the owner raises his hand in Spock-like greeting, his face impassive. Not until a piece of laundry falls from our balcony onto the power lines below do we learn that this man is in fact our downstairs neighbor. His wife lends us a laundry pole to poke at the pants tangled in the mess of cables, our attempts punctuated by the golden retriever's barks. We do manage to get the wayward trousers in the end.

—

Every day is an adventure here, even when I'd really prefer not to have an adventure that day. Today we wake up and there's sunlight and dust streaming in through a gaping hole in the wall behind our kitchen sink. (I can assure you this was NOT here yesterday.) They must have punctured through the plaster while doing renovations on the adjacent building. The construction workers instruct us to stick something through the hole to flag its location. I root around and finally settle on a cooking chopstick. They repair the hole, but we never get the chopstick back. I should have placed its mate alongside.

—

When T works on his dissertation, the wall by his right ear coos, coos, coos. It takes us a while to figure it out—there's a nook in the outer wall where a pigeon has decided to roost. Occasionally we'll hear what sounds like a hiccupping tokay inside the apartment. Many Cambodians are terrified of the geckos, but it's the cockroaches that have me screaming my head off.[*] There's the daybreak when, still half asleep, I begin pouring the contents of the electric kettle into our pitcher for purified water. At which point I notice the reddish-brown abomination[†] lounging on top of the water boiler.[**] The Buddhist boyfriend has to go out and reassure our neighbors that he has not murdered me.

---

[*] My parents suspect this katsaridaphobia stems from an exceptionally large representative of the species that torpedoed into my mosquito net one summer day in Shanghai, a year after I was born.

[†] Twitching antennae inches from my face!

[**] Are their f-ing footpads insulated? Steam is coming out of this kettle!!

—

One morning I jog past a deaf-mute teenager biking along the Tonle Sap. Arms waving like anemones in the hot-humid air, he sways and hums to a music all his own. His voice is eerie and elegiac. He dances right past the caged birds singing.

—

I miss being able to tell you these little things, inconsequential really, and yet there is something in their minuteness that sparkles, don't you think?

DEAREST,

I was driving today. Then I started talking to you like before when I could pick up the phone and call anytime. Suddenly I was crying and talking to you and driving all at once which I thought you would find pretty funny, especially since the boyfriend had used up all the Kleenex in the car (without replacing it—shocking, I know), so here I was, one big sniveling, chattering, snot-dripping, cackling, swerving mess.

Keep it together, lady, keep it together.

Remember when T told us he saw a great blue heron kill a gopher (thwack! the beak chiseling through the poor mammal's skull) and swallow it whole (gulp! the neck bulging like a grotesque Adam's apple) at the dried-up lake behind our dorm room? How we didn't believe him until several years later—why were we walking on a golf course, was it in Portland or Bend or Eugene, I can't remember because we were talking about kiwis (the bird, not the fruit) so that in my memory we were in New Zealand—when we see a great blue heron, whose preternatural stillness halts our conversation. We watch with bated breath until—thwack!

Whereupon we both start screaming, much to the amusement of the nearby golfers, who snicker, keep it together, ladies, it's just a bird.

I REALIZED TODAY THAT OUR friendship has been one long listening.

I'm still listening.

It feels like you are too.

I love you.

I miss you.

I WISH I COULD SHOW you where we're living now. Even though it's temporary because we'll be off to Thailand in the fall (T has a postdoc in Bangkok). Even though I think of it as his parents' home rather than our own. (Well, technically it is his parents' place.)

It's different than when we stationed here those seven months in grad school, after moving out of our cottage in the clouds, before we found the apartment in downtown Berkeley. The cottage was way too small but we would have stayed on if our sweet landlords Y and G hadn't had to unexpectedly sell the property. We still keep in touch with them, by the way. They're happily retired in Southern California, though they miss the Berkeley Hills. She makes jewelry, he does photography. They take K and D on long walks by the beach—remember how they sidled over when you visited us and gaped at the local co-op pizza in your hands with such mournful puppy-dog eyes that we all felt guilty eating our slices? Y and G would let us use their laundry machine even though it set the collies on high alert, raring to herd the intruders out. I still have a note in Y's cheerful handwriting. "We found your sock! Have a nice day!"

Like I was saying, it's different than when we were stationed here last. T's childhood bedroom is now his workspace and library, the walls wholly colonized by books, shelves sagging under the weight of those tomes. The music room has lost its untunable piano and is now my light-filled writing room looking out onto the garden. Our bedroom and bathroom lie on the corridor between our offices, cozy and cockroach-free, a major upgrade from Phnom Penh, though that sewer-scented apartment managed to maintain a certain charm in spite of its escalating decrepitude.

I run most weekday mornings at the trail by the reservoir nearby. You could dispatch the whole twelve miles—six each way—with ease, graceful as the deer lining the path, deer that slurp up mint-green moss draped like Dali clocks over low branches. I, however, lumber along to the 1.5-mile mark and huff my way back. I'm starting to recognize the regulars, like the elderly couple in matching pastel sweaters who are always holding each other's hands as they walk, a pair of Easter Peeps. They aren't the same regulars as five years ago. I especially miss Martin, who must have been a decade older than this couple, who would greet me with a new variation of my name every time we crossed paths. I want to think he's moved away, even if frailty or death are the more likely reasons for his absence.

I wonder if that group of septa- and octogenarians still gathers on Sunday mornings at our university bookstore in the upstairs café you frequented. They welcomed you into their club without reserve. You always had a special connection with the elderly—I think because of the way you possessed a joie de vivre undampened by looming mortality. When we went back to campus several years after graduation—was it the time you gave that speech, for bestowing the prize named in honor of your sister, whose alma mater you would come to share, who died of the same disease that would eventually claim your life too?—you were disappointed the coterie of seniors wasn't there, though one of the baristas (the one whose name rhymes with iguana) bounded toward you with a squeal of delight, then wrapped you in a big hug and asked if it was a mocha or regular-black-coffee-no-sugar-no-cream day.

You said, tell me about your world, then listened to all my parentheses and digressions, such that I could hardly imagine I was once a teenager who felt life to be an unbearable burden. Who would have guessed the way out was K's pining and D's pout, the reunion of a fuzzy sock with its mate, the robustness of Martin's wave? I wish I could tell you, on this morning's jog I saw a hummingbird on the trail, on that afternoon's walk a bunny, feeling my love for these little things burgeon upon your savoring of them too.

PS: ONLY JUST NOW NOTICED *how sisterly the two are, "listening" and "witnessing." In sound and in spirit.*

THE HOSPITAL ID BADGE PINNED above my heart reads: Chenxing Han—Chaplain. The binder cradled in my arms elaborates: Chenxing Han—Spiritual Care 韩辰星 · 精神与心理关怀.

Other job titles come about more spontaneously.

On the oncology unit, a woman is dying, though much slower than the doctors predicted. In her coma of rasping breaths, hours become days become agonizing weeks. I meet the patient's beloved for the first time outside the room. Eyes ablaze, F assures me that her wife would emphatically *not* want a visit from a chaplain, could I refrain from going into the room?

I promise I won't go in. As our supervisors remind us, sometimes the greatest act of spiritual care is to give patients and their families the power to turn you away. Some do just that, screaming *get the hell out!* Which tends to go over less well with the doctor, nurse, social worker, occupational therapist, phlebotomist. We're happy to give people this modicum of choice when so much else is outside their control.

Following F's forceful request and my promise to honor it, we lapse into silence. Unsure how to proceed, I follow an instinct.

"Would you like a hug?"

Surprise in her gray-green eyes. A slow-motion nod.

I encircle F gently at first, but upon registering the fierceness of her reciprocating embrace, I squeeze her tight, feeling the rise and fall of her breath, the heave and heart of her sorrow, until she finally lets go, wipes her eyes, and sighs, *I needed that.*

After that, she calls me "the hugging lady." And that is what we exchange each time we cross paths, not words but hugs, until her wife dies.

FOR MY MASTER'S THESIS, I interviewed the Angry Asian Buddhist. My advisor made the introduction. How could I not speak to the pseudonymous blogger whose writing had inspired my research project in the first place? Our conversation outlasted my voice recorder's batteries. The recording bubbles with laughter. My interviewee had a gift for spinning a fine yarn.

For example: One dark evening in Illinois, the Angry Asian Buddhist gets stuck behind a slow driver on the winding two-lane road leading to his parents' house. "It's a forty-five-mile-an-hour road, and they're going, like, thirty. And I'm from Los Angeles at this point! I'm driving behind them so closely you can see my pores in the rearview mirror." The driver turns onto a side street. The very side street A was planning to take.

At which point he realizes his mother had gotten a new Camry.

This is the story that drove home for him[*] the pragmatic implications of acting on the Buddhist belief that everyone you encounter has been your mother in a previous life. Or, for the reincarnation skeptics out there, might be your mother in *this* life.

At another point in the interview, A characterizes his father as a temporary wanderer within Buddhism. Only as a young adult did his father adopt Buddhism on his own terms. (Of the perpetually smoky Buddhist altar that his grandmother kept in her bedroom closet, A laughs, "I don't know how it didn't burn the house down!") But love had another religion in store for the Angry Asian Buddhist's dad, who converted to Judaism after marrying the woman that would one day be tailgated home by her son.

I would think about that phrase during my chaplaincy residency, *the temporary wanderer within.* And I would think of it again when A got diagnosed with cancer at the age of thirty-three. Though his disease was exceedingly rare, he thought himself not so different than you or me. All of our lives will eventually—inevitably—end in death.

We are, all of us, temporary wanderers within.

Still, I can't help but think, two friends, two cancers, two years, two deaths.

Too young.

Too soon.

---

[*] In my defense, he could never resist a pun.

Dearest,

Oh, the wonders of modern videoconferencing technology, that I could see you in real time when it would have taken three flights and thirty-six hours to make it to your wedding. Your wedding less than two weeks after the diagnosis, your wedding exactly one week from when you were supposed to defend your master's thesis in counseling psychology.

I cried witnessing how completely you adored each other. But I'll admit I also thought, it wasn't supposed to be this way, I had blocked off four days in October to be in Oregon, I was about to book my flight from Phnom Penh to Portland, my book draft was going to be done so it'd be doubly celebratory, you already had that show-stopping length of French silk ready to be made into the gown you'd never dreamed of, never dreamed of because as a girl you said died instead of passed away and carried a life expectancy that rendered veils and trains and silhouettes and sequins irrelevant.

I am angry. Our talismans have failed us. The cancer would not have cared whether the plane tickets were a mouse click away or stored in my phone or printed out in triplicate on multicolored onionskinny carbon paper, would not have cared that the silk was fair trade and the dress to be locally made by seamstresses earning a living wage. The tickets, the dress: like Bullwinkle. Ritual implement, magic staff: powerful but capricious. Conduit of care but no guarantor against death.

Best-laid plans go awry.

YOUR BROTHER CALLS IT ALCHEMY. *Happenstance that thumbs its nose at probability, juts its tongue at logic. Encounters, shimmering-strange, that dissolve the grief or anger or numbness of a moment-eternity ago. Instances surreal & numinous & awestruck.*

My high school ex would call it synchronicity, but you can probably understand why I prefer not to use that word, given that autumn afternoon freshman year when you and I were still getting to know each other and I was whacking the shit out of a ten-pound bar of chocolate with a butcher knife after a distressing encounter with the aforementioned ex. A moment revisited by us many a time since with chortling (ok, maybe a touch maniacal) glee.

SHE WAS THE ONLY PATIENT during my residency year to ask for a radio. I visited three of our chaplaincy department's offices before unearthing one, the black plastic furred with dust, the cassette deck frozen with age. But it's portable, it has an FM dial, it will do.

She tears up the moment I plug it in. There's no need to change the dial. The jazz is crystal clear.

"My father and I used to listen to this station." She wipes her eyes. "He died recently."

Drum riff. "It's a way to feel connected to your father," I note.

She nods. "Saturdays are my favorite. This is not my favorite DJ . . ."

The sound crackles to static.

"He heard you! It stopped!"

We laugh. When she leaves the hospital a few days later, I collect the radio. Alchemy has loosened its maw. I walk to the chaplaincy office with a spring in my step, my revived companion grinning for a tape, ready to sing a thousand songs.

L*OVE*,

Remember when you were debating whether to go to DC, and that handsome man you were dating (future fiancé, but we didn't know that yet) was headed to a conference and had asked you to come along, and I got so excited about you going that I wouldn't relent, until laughing you promised you'd book the flight as soon as we got off the phone, and you did and you were so glad you went?

So your mom and I are going to Maui.

Did you put us up to this?

Because first, there was the dress.

I was at the monastery in Taiwan when your boyfriend proposed. I do not think my shrieks of joy were in keeping with the decorum of the dormitory. "This was NOT part of my life script. But it is really great, Chenxing. I am really, deeply happy. Surprised, but really, deeply happy." I felt in that moment an unstoppable torrent of happiness for you.

So this is what they mean by mudita and its boundlessness. Another one of those brahmaviharas, mindstates sublime, dwellings divine.

When after ten-plus years the Buddhist boyfriend becomes my fiancé, I imagine the phone call I would have made: you shrieking with excitement, then saying oh, love in a way that would make me cry because you've borne witness to every step of our journey, the finding & loving & losing & finding & loving again.

Isn't it funny how a new status doesn't-but-does change things? I feel guilty, now that he and I are [use pretentious French accent here] fiancé(e)s, for not going to New York and Boston to see the US premier of Bangsokol, A Requiem for Cambodia (for which the fiancé wrote the libretto). My wardrobe, which fits into a single suitcase, consists almost entirely of clothing appropriate only for 30–40°C (86–104°F) weather, which is to say, my dishabille prevents me from surviving two weeks of East Coast winter. Also, I am trying desperately to establish a writing schedule.

T goes off to New York, gives a talk at Columbia, buses over to Cornell to peer at manuscripts through frozen eyelashes, buses back to NYC to watch the requiem, fails to notice Angelina Jolie at the reception afterward, decides to buy me a ticket *so I can see the show in Boston. His parents have gone to New York with him but are skipping the Massachusetts leg. When I pick them up from SFO his mom hands me her thickest coat, the one she bought for a winter trip to Russia. I spend my four days in Boston ensconced in this mummy sleeping bag. Going up the stairs of the subway, I have to hoist up the sides like the train of a wedding gown.*

But I digress. Where was I? Oh, right! The dress.

I SAW YOUR BROTHER LAST WEEK—for the first time since your memorial, I realized with a start.

Walking by the creek near my favorite climbing gym, we reflect on your death, eucalyptus leaves crunching underfoot. His voice is matter-of-fact. "When she died, a part of me died too." He pauses. "She had been a witness to so much of my life." And he to the full span of yours, from golden infancy to gleaming young adulthood, from first shaky steps to last quake of breath.

He tells me your mom is going to be in town for the weekend. They're going to a vegan potluck Sunday evening, an evening that might include some guided meditation. I can't pass up an opportunity to see your mom. Even if it means I have to meditate.

I arrive promptly at six—that should leave me enough time to drive back across the bridge, pack my bags, catch a few winks before waking up at four in the morning to head to Boston in the mummy sleeping bag. I'm wearing the only pair of meditation-appropriate pants I own: baggy, formerly purple, dyed black so I wouldn't be mistaken for a walking eggplant at the Buddhist college in Taiwan— distinctly unsexy. I expect to be greeted by a roomful of casually attired animal rights activists, your brother's tribe.

The bearded man in thick spectacles who answers the doorbell several minutes after I ring it—during which time I wander the hallway and squint at the gilded numbers of the adjacent apartments, wondering if I have the wrong address— looks utterly baffled. He doesn't know who I am, doesn't recognize your brother's name, but welcomes me in anyway as the first guest of the evening.

There will be no meditation at this holiday party, for which I am totally underdressed. You can imagine my mounting distress as my texts and calls to your brother go unanswered. Half an hour, then an hour, passes as the room fills with beautifully bedecked people, none of whom know your brother. I'm trying to gather, from snippets of conversation among this retinue of strangers, biographical details about this party's host. A beloved teacher of Advaita Vedanta, which explains the Hindu art. He's legally blind, which explains the alphabetized spice rack in the chai-perfumed kitchen.

Somehow I don't think you'd be surprised that your brother hasn't arrived yet.

Finally—finally!—*he materializes, in a rush of hugs and apologies, and of course it is impossible to stay exasperated at him (you know).*

And then your mom is there.

We hug for a long, long, long time, neither of us wanting to let go.

BOUNDARIES ARE A TRICKY THING to navigate as a chaplain. There is the man who says with a broken-toothed smile, "I find you attractive." His gnarled hand with the two missing fingers, casualties of severe diabetes, creep toward my knee. I consider making a beeline for the door, but grit my teeth, scoot out of arm's reach, and redirect the conversation instead.

It always surprises me how often chaplains are blessed. I thought I'd be doing all the blessing.

Steered away from come-ons, the man relates the pockmarked road of his life, his attempts at treading a godly path. He prays, *may the Buddha bless you and may God bless you.* He recalls an aunt who used to take him to church.

"What happened to her?" I ask.

"She came around less often, and I had to grow into missing her."

I TELL YOUR MOM THAT the Buddhist boyfriend and I are finally (it only took a decade) getting married. Her eyes light up in delight, then darken with urgency.

"Darling."

"Yes?"

"Do you have a dress?"

"Oh, no, not yet, I probably wasn't going to look until summer."

I figure I'll get something off the rack, probably not in white, certainly not from a bridal shop.

SHE OFFERS ME YOUR DRESS.

I AM TRYING TO KEEP it together.

    I am not succeeding.

    It is so hard, this growing into missing you.

WHO AMONG US DARES, REALLY *dares, to confront reality? The truth is, all that is dear to us can be wrenched away at any moment. Guts clench and hearts heave at the mere thought.*

Somehow, you dared:[*]

> If I were to die tomorrow, would I be content with the life I've lived? I have asked myself this question since childhood—a bedtime practice likely inspired by losing the precious sisters who shared my illness so early in life. The answer has always been an unequivocal yes. Fanconi anemia has represented a constant invitation to reflect on what really matters to me (love, nature, presence, gratitude) and has enriched my life in unexpected, deeply meaningful ways.

I tried to pray as an elementary student in Pennsylvania, parroting what they taught us in a weeklong Christian summer camp where we had to recite, before meals: god is great, god is good, let us thank him for our food, by his hands we all are fed, give us lord our daily bread. *It confused me, why god got demoted from great to good in the span of a breath, why our cafeteria lunches of rubbery ham sandwiches and mushy apples were worthy of thanks, why people would eat bread and not rice every day.*

More intriguing was: now I lay me down to sleep, I pray the lord my soul to keep, if I should die before I wake, I pray the lord my soul to take. *Though here too, problems. What soul? For that matter, what lord? And come to think of it, would this invocation increase my likelihood of getting snatched away by this variably great/good god?*

At the vegan potluck holiday party hosted by the bespectacled Advaita Vedanta teacher, your brother tries to explain the concept of anatman *to a longtime friend, the one your family has known forever, the dude whose Oregonian lumberjack-in-flannel getup belies his white-collar consulting job in San Francisco.*

"You know this thing you think is your self? It's not—and it's not forever," your brother enthuses.

---

[*] *Also the Buddha. Though that was a long time ago.*

His bear of a friend mulls this over. A long silence.

"That's fucked up, man," the lumberjack-bear-friend deadpans, and we can't help but laugh.

He waits for our merriment to subside before continuing.

"Seriously though—I can't imagine not seeing my family again."

YOUR MOTHER HAS BEEN DOGGEDLY *calling the dress studio.*

Your mother is a force of nature (you know). This is a woman who worked in Côte d'Ivoire in the sixties, advocated for children as a clinical social worker before raising five of her own, cofounded with her husband the first and only research fund for a disease that would kill all three of their daughters.

Fifteen months before she is hounding the studio, as we stand next to each other in the hospital waiting room, I confess to your mom the dismal state of my Khmer. She advises that I yammer away as loudly as possible to everyone I meet, making LOTS of mistakes because how else am I going to learn the language? I nod in agreement, though I want to point out that some of us have inherited a teaspoon of gumption to the gallon she got.

HER LAST DAUGHTER IS DYING AND YOUR MOTHER *is asking me for book recommendations. We stand shoulder to shoulder in the hospital waiting room watching Chad ferry people from the waterfront to this castle in the sky. Wan faces smile at us from the anodyne covers of cancer brochures.* I am hesitant to recommend a book I've just read, Vaddey Ratner's* In the Shadow of the Banyan, *told from the perspective of a seven-year-old girl living in 1970s Cambodia whose father, a poet, is murdered by the Khmer Rouge.*

I was reading Han Kang's The Vegetarian *when H called about your diagnosis. Of those dark days I remember only chopped, howling nightmares—a Korean woman transmogrified into a tree.*

In my first email to you post-diagnosis, subject line "Beauty," I tell you I'm reading In the Shadow of the Banyan. *"I was inspired by the book's message to look for beauty always—which of course makes me think of you—and I wanted to send you an image of beauty from today." Hence the fuchsia flowers. In later emails, the dragonscale buttermilk sky above the National Museum. Sunset from the Pompidou in Paris. Plush Bernese mountain dog and capybara at Harrod's. Real live bushy-tailed fox in a Bangkok coffee shop.*

Your mother loves the book, devours it in all its devastation. Fifteen months later, she's still giving rave reviews. Animated, she relates the unthinkable tragedies little Raami had to endure to a new friend at the holiday party while an hors d'oeuvres spread away your brother earnestly explains anatman to a befuddled man in flannel. In Maui, your mom prepares to lead a discussion for her book club about the young Cambodian girl's heartrending plight.

---

* *Exemplars of the sorry-your-tail's-been-drooping-a-little genre*

THE DAY YOUR MOM WRITES *to tell me there's a studio in Portland ready to make my wedding dress, I get another email advertising low fares to Hawaii.*

I never get spam anymore (confession: I block that shit with a vengeance rivaled only by my stance on cockroach extirpation). How did this sneak through?

You know how OCD I am. I know, I should say "highly organized," "detail-oriented," but let's be real, it got worse in Cambodia after your diagnosis, worse still after I went back to Phnom Penh after seeing you for the last time in Oregon. My inbox has been at zero ever since, an empty crypt. With no tomb to sweep, I scour my messages, clear them constantly, as if to prepare the purest possible place for a missive from you to arrive. Or maybe it is that if I see only blank space on this screen I won't think about what isn't there because a whole lifetime without another email or card or letter or text or phone call from you is as unthinkable as not doing four to seven loads of laundry a week (hanging it all up by hand, like my nainai used to do) and logging every book I read three ways (social cataloging website, bibliographic management software, electronic spreadsheet) and tracking every item of clothing I own (photo gallery, twelve-column two-hundred-sixty-eight-row table: leave no sock unaccounted, record whence this bra came, log what these undies are made of).

But there it is, a photo of Hawaii. Beige sand, brown rocks, turquoise waves, white surf, marigold sun, pink-purple sky, green palms. I know how much you loved Hawaii. Where your boyfriend proposed while your mom was so engrossed in scuba diving she missed the big moment, forcing you to restage your elation for her tardy camera lens. In defense of her obliviousness, you were pretty clueless too, even when the ring box protruded conspicuously from his running shorts, even when it fell out and he had to retrieve it, even when he drew a circle in the sand and you thought yay, fun, a circle, let's jump in!

Anyway, I have the urge to forward this email to your mom. If I never get spam, I never, ever forward it to anyone. Screw it. Tackiness be damned. The fares from Portland (and San Francisco) are so cheap, wouldn't this bring a minute's amusement, a silly diversion, on a dark winter day in Oregon?

YOUR MOM WRITES BACK IMMEDIATELY. "*Hawaii. Wouldn't it be just wonderful to spend a bit of time there? I would really love that! Would you seriously have the time for such a trip, and if so, when might that be? I am actually tempted!*"

This was NOT the reply I expected. At most, I thought she might want to go on her own, though it seemed unlikely. Your mom's been so busy with the research fund she can't even remember the last time she stole away for a long weekend. I certainly never thought she'd suggest going to Hawaii together.

I CAN'T BELIEVE WE ARE *thinking about doing this.*

Two seats left on this flight, 3 percent of accommodations remain, sorry we are out of rental cars. I get those two seats, your mom nabs a condo, I find a different rental car company. It takes us three days to arrange everything for our week in Maui.

After booking our condo, your mom realizes it's right by the beach where you got engaged.

She writes, "I woke up this morning with a big smile on my face just thinking that we are actually going to do this! Wow."

You once said you felt all of life was conspiring toward your happiness.

For the longest time, I couldn't honestly say I understood. But I am starting to get a glimmer of what you mean.

WHEN THE BUDDHIST FIANCÉ AND I finally get married, at the open space preserve where tree-wave upon tree-wave unfurls to the ocean, my father bawls through the entire ceremony, from processional to poem to 南無本師釋迦牟尼佛 to *all my ancient twisted karma* to Pali refuges and precepts to poem to vows to rings to mala bracelets to きんす to poem to 南無觀世音菩薩 to metta to recessional with tatami-scented wind at our backs.

I imagine them to be the tears he never shed at the funeral for his father that he never attended.

Two years later, when I muster up the courage to ask, Dad says no, no, it's not that. I couldn't stop crying because I was just too happy.

DO YOU REMEMBER THAT ADVANCED *yoga class we went to, when the instructor, a wizened but spry Indian man, paused at my mat while surveying our forward folds, then pushed and pushed until my torso and legs became a pressed panini? I think I may have squeaked. I definitely heard you growl. You were ready to tackle him, you told me later. We have been mama bears to each other, though when oceans separated us I had to send an elephant in my stead on wish-winds of metta.*

You, fierce friend, orchestrated a birthday celebration for your mama from your hospital bed. Among the multiple gifts: a massage that you know she needs, she who can hardly bear to leave your side. In your journal you write, "Ask that your caretakers care for themselves, and then trust that they will do so."

REMEMBER WHEN YOU WERE PLANNING *your nuptials and wanted ten people on your side of the wedding party and your mama said that was far too unwieldy, then balked at your backup plan of shrinking the entourage to just two bridesmaids: your brothers?*

I said, oh, love, I'm sorry it's been so stressful—but . . . what's a wedding party? Isn't a wedding a kind of party? So why not just say wedding? Or party(-where-there-is-going-to-be-an-elegant-white-dress-and-possibly-a-veil-and-definitely-a-tiered-cake-but-heightened-pomp-and-circumstance-aside-isn't-it-in-essence-just-like-any-other-party)? "Wedding party" is a bit redundant, don't you think?

In my defense, my parents' wedding consisted of dinner with a handful of friends at their Shanghai apartment. Everyone wore pants.

My question cracked you up. By the time you'd explained bridesmaids and maids of honor and groomsmen and best mans to me, you'd forgotten about the impossible task of choosing a wedding party that would appease everyone.

*W*HEN *I* TELL MY FUTURE *mother-in-law about how your wedding dress has become mine, a pinched look crosses her face. This is not a household where tears reign freely, and suddenly I am* 鼻酸 *too, a squeeze of lemon in the nose.* Oh, that makes me want to cry, *she says, and I sniffle,* I know, me too.

Your mama gets last-minute instructions for her sister-in-law's wedding. The women of the family (who are part of the wedding party!—exercising my new-found vocabulary, hell yeah) are asked to wear blue dresses. This is not welcome news. Your mom doesn't have a blue dress, or the time to get one. Your husband, whose attention to detail clearly extends beyond the hospital pharmacy where he works, remembers there is a dress in the basement draped over a chest of your clothing. You bought that dress for your cousin's wedding, which you weren't able to attend. But you are a petite 00, two sizes smaller than your mom. She's convinced there is no way it will fit.

Of course, it fits. Of course, she looks stunning in it.

Do I detect a gleam in your eye?

THE KOREAN WOMAN IS TURNING into a tree the tree is turning into a pillar of light you are leaving the blackwater woods call me walk through the woods once more this time in the dark your castle in the sky chad asleep bullwinkle spent in a room you've left behind your family gathered round if i have a soul that is what is being called love i know it is time to go i will be ok it is more than enough i have held you to my bones because my life depended on it now it is time to let you go we are born to go love comes so the korean woman is turning into a tree the tree is turning into a pillar of light you are leaving the blackwater woods call me walk through the woods once more this time in the dark your castle in the sky chad asleep bullwinkle spent in a room you've left behind your family gathered round if i have a soul that is what is being called love i know it is time to go i will be ok it is more than enough i have held you to my bones because my life depended on it now it is time to let you go we are born to go love comes so

PART VI: 沧海桑田

sea change

THE COLLAGE SHE MADE FOR me hangs on the wall of the guest bedroom at my parents' house, kitty-corner from the Buddha statues still on the dresser. The collage's border is in her signature style, a clockwise wraparound of found words. In this case, a single found image as well, of a slipper chair upholstered in red velvet. Sometimes I allow my eyes to circumambulate this perimeter until it becomes a mantra:

> Pull up a—[here the chair]—and—**CREATE**—TIME—love—sing—play—write—*laugh.*—HUG—HAVE ENGAGING CONVERSATIONS—learn—live—simply—Be—*present*—Pull up a . . .

At the center, a quote from her favorite artist-poet, copied in a handwriting that is stylized yet unmistakably hers:

"In the end,

I think that I will

like

that we were

sitting on the bed,

talking

& wondering where

the time had gone."

—*Kai Skye*

ON THE EVE OF GRADUATION, we were sitting not on the bed but the floor, knowing this would be the last time we would live in adjacent bedrooms. The week a whirlwind of scheduled celebrations, assiduously designed to bypass the cavern of loss that underfurs every major transition.

"Every day is bonus to me," she confided.

I cried then, not only at the prospect that those bonus days would run out, but for all the times I had considered truncating my own. The hubris my health had spawned. The hours my self-loathing had spurned. How she with the truly abbreviated future could live with such purpose and gratitude, deliberateness and spontaneity, while I wallowed in directionless doubt, unwilling to partake in the give-and-take, the work-and-play, of creating a future I could call happy.

"Promise me you won't ever kill yourself," she demanded.

FIVE AND A HALF YEARS later, I would remember that I'd promised. It was just before her father died. A time when I couldn't burden her with more. The despair returned, creeping then crushing, alongside a cacophony of surreal, destabilizing, traumatic events.

I thought of our conversation on the dorm room floor, and then I thought of the hardworking hospital staff, the patients they cared for, the families who worried about those patients. I thought of how they expected me back the next day. Nurse C would miss my morning greeting (and I hers: "Keep smilin', honey, it's contagious"). The valet parking attendants would miss a chance to rib me ("Easy money today, chaplain?"). R would miss being heard. F would miss being hugged.

The hospital that has invited me into its peculiar community, its complicated ecosystem, becomes the haven where I keep my promise. Patients bless me when we pray together. The security staff vow to watch out for my stalker. My supervisors let me count the court date as a work day. The hearing ends with the victory of a restraining order at the expense of my dignity. My peer group listens when I tell them how everything has fallen apart, I am dead tired, I don't think I can go on. They listen and say they will miss me if I quit the residency and when someone starts to give advice I plead with them to just be with me in the shittiness of it all.

And so they do. They sit with tears in their eyes. They don't try to fix a thing. The mercy of it.

The Buddha says, *oh, no, Ananda, admirable friendship is not half of the holy life—it is the whole of it.*

Of all that she left for me—cards and letters, collages and a wedding dress—here is the inheritance I cherish most: the understanding that every day is bonus. In time, even the sadness is a kind of pining salve. Even the grief a mossy gift.

I REREAD THE FINAL EMAILS she sent me.

"*I just love you so much it makes me cry.*"

"*Thank you for the photos, the love, the snippets of life from where you are.*"

"*I can't believe you made it on time [to our videoconference wedding]. It filled my heart to see you.*"

"*THERE IS A FOX THERE IS A FOX IN THOSE PHOTOS AND IT IS BLOWING MY MIND IS IT REAL? A PET?*"

"*I just want to keep writing that I love you.*"

"*Also I read your article and it is AMAZING. So proud of you, admire you like crazy, and love you like nobody's business.*"

"*I love that the title of our email strain is Beauty. Such an important reminder right now. My window is east-facing, so I have been enjoying that morning scene very much :).*"

"*Also I just really can't believe you found a stuffed Bernese mountain dog and capybara . . . that is beyond amazing and the photo warms my heart completely.*"

"*I love you and I love the elephant you sent. I am almost completely away from email but I want you to know that your love and support is so deeply felt.*"

"*Love love love,*"

I wonder if there will ever be a day when I won't weep reading these words.

Maybe it's ok if that day never comes.

It's as she used to say, I just love you so much it makes me cry.

IN THE END, SHE WAS transferred to the ICU for difficulty breathing. In the end, there was no time to move the entire gallery of greeting cards, but the elephant stood guard at the entrance of her new room. In the end, the ICU waiting room filled with family and friends wanting a last audience. In the end, we were sitting on the (hospital) bed, talking (only a little, to spare her the effort) and wondering where (and how) the time had gone (so quickly). Her mom and I flanked her tiny frame, finding easy purchase on the narrow bed that she occupied so little of.

She asked us to massage her aching soles. We peeled away the compression socks. Rubbed warmth and lotion into her feet, cold and dry but still elegantly pedicured. My first and last time touching her feet.

It was hard to leave the room, but her soles were soothed and there was a queue of other visitors. It was harder still to leave the hospital, though by then she was asleep.

I JOLT AWAKE AT 3 a.m. a forest between us she is leaving the monastery on the hill 一路顺风 slipping away before the first light before the text message that will sink our friend who is named for sunrise to her knees

NOW THAT SHE'S DEAD, WHO will share my delight over grief banks? She who wouldn't be surprised that the first article I flip to in this week's *New Yorker* is about a young graduate of our alma mater who dies of a brain tumor, playing music to the very end. Who else will love these *samvega*-laced discoveries? Now that she's dead, no one listens as she did.

I blunt my listening to the world. Retribution.

The CPE supervisor from a nearby hospital, while guest speaking on bereavement, drew us a grief bank. Triangle roof, square base, rectangle door. A dead ringer for the houses I used to draw as a child, except there are no 田 for windows. For years after coming to America, I would draw, ad infinitum, exactly four things: 1) those houses, and beyond the fields of their windows, 2) cats, 3) dogs, 4) piranha-toothed fish. When I reunite with my childhood nanny in Shaoxing as a teenager, a decade after our last embrace, I sketch that quadriptych of images for her. She drops the blow dryer in shock.* "They're exactly like the ones I taught you to draw," she exclaims. "They were the only four things I knew how to draw!" When we visit Lu Xun's former residence the next morning, people stop us to ask if I am her daughter. We beam: you could say that.

We make deposits and withdrawals to this grief bank all our lives. The visiting chaplain stands with his marker poised in front of the whiteboard. *The favorite blankie you lost when you were five:* he draws a square inside the bank-hut. *Your friend calls you fat in third grade:* another square. *Mittens dies:* another square. *Actually, on second thought . . .* he adds another square for Mittens. *Grandpa gets sick*—another square—*grandpa dies*—more squares. *Your first breakup, you don't get into the college of your dreams, you get laid off*—if the squares were bales, not a single horse would fit in this barn, though you could feed it for months.

Fortunately, grieving—doleful as the process may be—has the very important function of removing the bales. Our presenter pantomimes walking through the door and carrying out one of the cubes, then erases it from the board. Drug addiction is like barring the door—the deposits are accumulating

---

* For those five days together, she insists on this nightly ritual, refuses to let me go to bed with wet hair, insists on wielding the hair dryer on my damp locks herself.

but the ability to withdraw them is so hampered that the newly sober may feel flattened by a ton of bricks from a backlog of, say, twenty numb years. The cumulative effect matters. A young boy whose mother has died of cancer may appear to be taking it in stride—but then he will see a butterfly crushed against the pavement and be utterly inconsolable.

My bank is full, the nurses at this chaplain's hospital will sometimes say, and find themselves met with greater gentleness, extra empathy.

WHO ARE YOU BECOMING NOW, *after my death?* She would ask me this, I'm sure. She would ask me, *How is the grieving?*

I would tell her, *Sometimes I feel so angry at the listening-bereft world that it hurts to talk to anyone who isn't you.* Which, inconveniently, is everyone.

I am angry because I want to talk to HER, specifically her, and there is only everyone else. I am furious that no one listens like she did. I am livid that it has become so hard for *me* to listen. A scrim of fury occludes my every interaction. In Phnom Penh it is almost a relief to fail at learning the language, to bury myself in parroted greetings and seething silences.

I know she would nod and assure me, *This is part of the process.* I know she would also nudge me: *Love, this cloak of bitterness does not become you.* It's not that she would want me sweeter, just that there are so many more flavors in this wild world of ours to savor.

WHO AM I BECOMING AFTER her death?

—a repeating question exercise

Thank you. Who are you becoming . . .

—a compulsive who can be undone by a missing sock (ankle, blue and white stripes, purchased in kyoto, 100% cotton)

Thank you. Who are you becoming . . .

—a dash of bitters, a backslash of anger

Thank you. Who are you becoming . . .

—a chaplain no longer, though there are still moments of chaplaining

Thank you. Who are you becoming . . .

—a writer maybe, like "chaplain" a strange thing to *be,* all i can say for certain is i have been writing

Thank you. Who are you becoming . . .

—a cicada abandons all crust of former self, yet is indelibly shaped by her previous moldings

Thank you. Who are you becoming . . .

THERE IS A MAN OF few words who has stayed on the oncology unit many months. His wife is not one to wear her emotions on her sleeve, though her daily presence speaks volumes. She is compact against his mountainous frame, which remains assuredly solid in spite of multiple rounds of chemo. The cancer has puffed his lips, swollen his face, enlarged his head, diminished his body—but it has not erased the kindness in his eyes, the gentleness of his smile, the peaceful curve of his ear.

Mr. C's signature gesture lets us know he is A-OK. His right arm lifts turtle-slow from the bed. His forefinger and thumb form a ring with the leisure of a summer cloud coalescing. His remaining three fingers stand at chivalrous attention with a slight bow at the waist. He will not live to see white supremacists ruin this gesture.

The presenter who drew us the grief bank remarks that every chaplain has an individual resting temperature. He asks us to register our personal thermometers. Do we run warm or cool, shy or overbearing, emotional or analytical, formal or casual, chatty or taciturn? Do we flee conflict or feed it?

Around Mrs. C, my temperature runs shy. She is always so poised, handbag tucked beneath her elbow as she walks calmly into her husband's room and decorously takes a seat. This room her house of worship, this chair her pew. Her reserve renders me more timorous than usual, as if tiptoeing around a sleeping swan.

The Cs are there so long they become, like K in her star-studded room, residents rather than visitors. Even the shyest of neighbors become familiar with each other. One day, I finally work up the courage. I intercept Mrs. C in the hallway before she steps into the room.

"I don't mean to bother you . . ." I begin. "Oh, you're never bothering me," she exclaims.

Out of earshot of her beloved, she explains. *I didn't want to let my guard down here at the hospital, but some days I go home and just* weep. *I never get angry at God, but sometimes I ask,* Lord, *whatcha doin', why you put this one on me?* She chuckles through her tears. She tells me about the loved ones she has already lost. Her brother: "I miss him to this day." A daughter who was my age: "Even though it's been twenty years, sometimes the grief is as fresh as the day she died."

In the span of a single conversation, civility blossoms into closeness, nourished by the loam of goodwill from months of simple greetings.

I am with Mrs. C and a few of her family members when the palliative care doctor lets them know that while Mr. C may still be here by the end of the week, he probably will not be with us by the end of the month. I witness them taking in the news. We bow our heads. There is nothing to fix. Let us be present in the remaining days.

HE ASKED FOR YOU, Mrs. C tells me. I walk in unable to speak, not even to ask *how is today?* Brown eyes big, mahogany hands soft—I expect those hands to take on their usual gesture. Instead, they grasp mine. My hands disappear in the enormity of his.

Time collapses. It is ten years ago, a hospital room in Shanghai. Like Mr. C, my uncle knows: this will be the last time. My dad's older brother, whom I've always called by the Shandarin portmanteau of Dababa, the first syllable Mandarin, the last two syllables staccato in an approximation of the Shanghainese, as if he were just a bigger version of my dad, a 大爸爸, though my disapproving Chinese school teacher would correct the characters to 大伯伯.

I am trying to smile through my terror. Shocked to see him without the thick mop of hair he's always had. Horrified when my cousin who is only three years older than me must spoon-feed mashed banana to her dying father. Paralyzed by the sour smell that threatens to obliterate all the warm memories I have of this monumental man.

Suddenly he pulls me into his signature bear hug, squeezing me tighter and longer than ever before, and in that silent eternity his fierce embrace declares that nothing, not cancer, not death, can erode the force of his love.

大爸爸 and Mr. C, before the frail monuments of their bodies crumble, press into mine the magnitude of their goodness, a song without words. The care that flows between us is not lost. *Carry this forth, child. Amplify it.*

Later there will be time to weep, and weep, and weep.

SOMETHING ELSE WRITING AND CHAPLAINING share in common: magic. From empty hands, something. More than something: whole worlds.

Chaplaining, writing: where extravagance and necessity meet. The final foot massage. A finger pointing to the moon. A thousand and one remember-whens. Arabian nights of tears pooling into a kalpa of oceans of remember-whens. Crossing to the other shore on swells of gratitude.

AT THE CONFERENCE WHERE A *five-year-old boy tried to beat me up, there were many Asian Buddhist women but few Asian American ones. At the meditation retreat with a plethora of teas, Asian Americans were also few and far between. Perhaps this is why I would misremember her, this woman from the Bay Area who shared your first name. When we finally reconnect, she corrects me: we met half a decade ago in Bangkok, not Northern California.*

You wrote from your hospital bed, "Hi love, just wanted you to know that I very much signed, any news?" Your name-twin organized the petition you signed. When I saw that she had been harmed by the same person* in different ways, I tried to get in touch. I couldn't find her email, and we weren't yet friends on social media, so my message got buried.

She sees my message the day before you died. "It's been a roller coaster," she tells me. "Traumatic really. Things keep popping back up, like the cords are not completely finished.† I would love to see you. One to chat and just catch up. Two I'd love to give you something to give Rev. B.** And if you are down for it, I'd love to do a healing ritual with you around this collective trauma. I do energy work now and would love to do a collective clearing."

Two days later I flew back from Portland at daybreak. My future mother-in-law opened the door. Oh, oh, she clucked, wrapping me in her arms as I sobbed.

I slept until it was time to meet your name-twin. We caught up over lunch at a Burmese restaurant.

A week later we built a bonfire by the beach, where I stood face-to-face with others who had been harmed by that same person in different ways.

A week after that she gave me a gift to take back to Cambodia for Rev. B.

Your memorial the following week. This time I fly back from Portland with a cardboard cylinder. Inside, bones burned to ash. Outside, chartreuse humming-birds in shimmering flight.

---

* *Spiritual teacher, stalker*

† *I know what she means. Even two years after that season of duress, I can't make a clean cut from the cords of trauma, can't silence the chords of fear.*

** *Rev. B being the American Zen nun who lives in Phnom Penh and ran Brahmavihara, the organization that was first T's, then my introduction to Buddhist chaplaincy. You would have met her at our wedding, which she officiated.*

IN HER ADVANCE DIRECTIVE, SHE writes, "I believe the season after the death of a loved one is for the individuals left to grieve." Under OTHER WISHES: "If or when my death is judged imminent . . ." She asks for warmth and love for the journey across. "This may be through Reiki, heart energy, and music would be most welcome." In those final days, she asks her mom to read her favorite Mary Oliver poem, about loving what is mortal, holding it against your bones, letting it go, letting it go.

"I'd love to say my memorial should be a celebration—because my life has been one giant celebration in my mind." The program will say CELEBRAT-ING, with a photo of her in exuberant mid-leap, marathon running bib aproned over her belly, arms flung wide like a Siberian crane in flight.

Preparing a eulogy for her memorial, I come across an email she wrote six years before her death: "For me, always one of the most comforting parts of grieving was redefining who I was in absence of the person of whom I was letting go."

She had always prepared me to lose her.

It is hard to color her death comforting. And yet, as the seasons pass—as seasons are wont to do—I discover in her death a liberating permission, borne by a steady reminder: If every day is bonus, what are you making the boon of today?

HALF A YEAR AFTER HER death, a reporter from *Runner's World* tells me he is writing a feature on my former college roommate. Can he interview me?

We figure out the time difference between Phnom Penh and Oregon. The voice on the other end of the line is somber: "This must be hard for you to talk about."

To the contrary, it is a delight to remember this dearest of friends. I don't want his questions to stop. I finish the conversation in high spirits.

Five minutes later, the future fiancé finds me sobbing on the couch in a fetal position.

At which point I realize I am crying because of a *running magazine.* Me, who jogs a ten-minute mile on a good day!

I burst out laughing.

Later the reporter asks me to check his copy, ten bullet points of a sentence or two each. Number 5 reads: "You became a runner because of her. Although you were slow, she always encouraged you."

I'm pretty sure this would have cracked her up too.

Bonus points for bluntness? Though, ouch. I wish he would soften it a bit. How about: "You could never keep up with her, even though she was shorter than your already short 5-foot-3"?

"I DO NOT WISH MY ashes to be a burden. Please ask the following individuals (in addition to close family) if they would like to spread my ashes in places they love . . ."

Of the ten names on her list, three of us live in the Bay; another, our beloved college friend from Morocco, had boarded a plane from the East Coast an hour before her final breath. How were we to apportion the contents of the hummingbird container among the four of us?

Our friend who is named for sunrise looks online for small urns. By her own admission, attention to detail is not this friend's strong suit. When they arrive in the mail, she realizes the urns are barely taller than the length of her thumbnail. Oops.

Six months after our beloved friend's death, when I am back in America for another friend's wedding, the three of us who live in the Bay Area* meet at Lands End. We discuss how nice it would be to distribute her ashes on the beach.

Turns out the beach is windy.

Turns out, wind and controlled transfer of ashes are not mutually compatible, especially when the mouths of the receiving receptacles can barely swallow a tadpole.

So here we are at the crowded Lands End Lookout Visitor Center, peering through floor-to-ceiling glass at crashing ocean waves, huddled next to a food service tub overflowing with cappuccino-stained cups and crumb-littered plates, trying to look inconspicuous.

Keep it together, ladies, keep it together.

We buy a hot chocolate and pass it around, pretending to be tourists between nervous sips. None of the spoons are small enough for our task, so we settle for a wooden stirrer. One person holds a Lilliputian urn in each hand, another uses the stir stick to ferry our friend's ashes from the hummingbird container to the two thimbles, a third cups her hands beneath the whole operation to catch any wayward wisps.

We learn that ashes are more like wet sand than powdered sugar. Still, my memory of that seascape-surrounded morning is sweet, sweet.

---

* 1) Me 2) The sunrise friend and obtainer of tiny urns 3) The friend named for the season that precedes her favorite one

MISSION ACCOMPLISHED, WE HEAD FOR the wind-whipped beach. We spell out her name with seashells, enclose the cockle-formed letters inside a heart made of driftwood and pebbles and pinecones.

No, not a burden but an adventure. Among the three of us, we are already dreaming of where to take her ashes. Two are among the possibilities she listed in her advance directive:

- Santorini
- Ireland—always wanted to go there!

The third is Harry Potter land. We think she would approve.

Walking the sandy path back to the parking lot, I startle at a familiar face. She is with two friends of her own. *We just held a ceremony for your name-twin* is all I manage to say. She eyes the hummingbird container cradled in my arms. At the beach she will find her name, a collection of found objects soon to be swept back to sea.

I ASKED FOR A SIGN. I don't like to seem superstitious,* but I asked for a sign anyway.

I had tacked on a few days in Dublin to the end of a Europe trip with my parents. In London, we stopped to visit my cousin. Her two little ones gape at us, strange relatives who speak Shanghainese and Mandarin—but not British English—like their mama and baba. My cousin coaxes her children to eat. Who she has become after her father's death. The spoon, the mashed banana, the twelve years since.

At Gatwick Airport en route to Dublin, a few ounces of fine sticky powder, hummingbird-encased, glide right through the X-ray scanners without triggering alarm. I have the death and cremation certificates the airline requires, but they remain sealed in an Oregon-postmarked envelope inside my purple carry-on backpack.

No burden at all. But where to scatter her ashes?

The ocean beckons, but the coastal towns that guidebooks go giddy over are too distant for this brief trip. Howth comes to mind—I remember it from reading *Dubliners* in high school—but is this too plebeian a choice? Doesn't this special occasion—we always wanted to go, here we are at last—merit a more out-of-the-way location? Portstewart, Kinsale, Caherdaniel, Strandhill? Maybe I should come back here another time, plan this out more carefully, rent a car . . . ?

Personal specialty, file under "F": frenzy of worry, working myself up into.

Hence the desperation. Hence the asking for a sign.

---

* I know I'm not the only Asian American Buddhist who's sensitive about this.

THAT FIRST MORNING IN DUBLIN, I followed the canal west, not knowing where it would lead. Later I would look on a map and see I had run six miles. No wonder my knees burned.

The day she died, her oldest brother posted a video with this message:

> After a months-long valiant struggle, my dear sister succumbed to complications from leukemia early this morning. She was surrounded by her loving family when she passed and spent the last days of her life in the company of adoring friends and relatives.

> A couple weeks ago, she and I filmed a last-ditch video plea to pharmaceutical executives for drugs we thought might save her life, and though her particularly vicious brand of AML took her before that effort could bear fruit, her words excerpted here so clearly summarized her boundless compassion for the beings with whom she shared this life, her unflagging determination, and the poetry of her soul. I'll never forget you; sister, teacher, and friend beyond compare.

53,000 views. One of those views was after a late brunch in Portland, the restaurant emptied of customers except for three college friends. We crowd around a tiny phone screen while our waitress folds napkins into bassinets for silverware in the far corner. On screen, our recently departed friend is dabbing at her mascara, chuckling as she remarks, "I am crying like a madwoman." I am too, I have never cried this hard in public, I am ruining this napkin bassinet with snot and tears (good thing they're sturdy, and made for this purpose, no?).

"What do you want to do in the world?" her brother asks at the beginning of that last-ditch video.

"I want to accompany people on their paths towards wellness," she responds, hair shorn and peach fuzz just growing back in. She looks like a baby bald eagle, if eagles nested in hospital beds and gowned up in mint green. "I remember reading something about the word for compassion in Pali. . . . The idea behind metta is that you show lovingkindness by meeting the suffering of others with an unwaveringly open and loving heart. That's what I want to do—I want to be a part of the healing of the people in this world."

"Tell me about running," her brother urges.

"I like to always stay at a place where I *could* run a half-marathon if I really had to. Goodness knows why I would *have* to run a half-marathon . . ." Bullwinkle starts beeping in the background.

"You never know when you're gonna have to, you know, run half of twenty-six miles to tell the Athenians what's up," her brother points out.

"That's what I'm sayin'!"

"Didn't you run a marathon?" he prompts.

She wipes away tears. "I ran a marathon. It was a goal of mine in my under-graduate college career. And my sophomore year of college, I did it. I have this disease Fanconi anemia, my blood counts weren't perfect. My doctor was actually concerned about what running the length of a marathon would do. And sure enough, my blood counts fell right around training mile 18. My hemoglobin dropped into the 8s, and then it was veering toward the 7s. But I was so determined to run this marathon that I begged my doctors to let me do it, and he started giving me EPO shots. So!" She laughs "I guess I was kind of doping. BUT! I made it! I did all 26.2, baby."

FAMISHED AFTER THE CANAL-SIDE RUN, I stumble across a newly opened café whose name evokes two of her favorite things, the nectar of bees and the fruit of cocoa trees. A kaleidoscope of colors glistens on my plate, six different vegetarian salads of the day. Pink marshmallows float in a mug of steamy milk and melted ganache—hot chocolate done right.

Here we are still sitting and talking, laughing and wondering where the time has gone.

The bus stop is just a few blocks away. I hop on the double-decker bound for Howth summit, admiring the view from my upper-deck front-row seat as we wend our way north. It is cold and drizzly when I disembark at a place that is more hillock than summit. I make a hesitant 360. Through the gloomy gray, I hear but can't see the ocean five hundred feet below.

A magnificent double rainbow blooms in the sky. I burst into tears.

IN A FLASH, A REMEMBRANCE of rainbows past.

Tibet literally breathtaking, the cutting colors, my gasping breaths. On a jeep ride to Shigatse, I look back at the expansive plateau. Etched in the illimitable sky, a double rainbow, contoured as stained glass. It remains suspended, a vividness that refuses to wane. Four months later, when my gap year has ended and college is beginning, I will meet a frosh named for sunrise. Our friendship is inevitable after we learn that we were journeying over the same roads under the same rainbow-lit sky at exactly the same time. She is the one who introduces me to her dormmate from Oregon.

For a few frantic days during sophomore year, we thought this dormmate needed a bone marrow transplant. Junior year, transplant averted, she shares an apartment with me on the east side of campus. The Buddhist not-yet-boyfriend sees a rainbow outside our balcony and admires it until it fades. He sets a poem by Saint John of the Cross to music and sings the words in a voice graveled by melancholy:

> I was sad one day and went for a walk;
> I sat in a field.
>
> A rabbit noticed my condition and
> came near.
>
> It often does not take more than that to help at times—
>
> to just be close to creatures who
> are so full of knowing,
> so full of love
> that they don't
> —chat,
>
> They just gaze with
> their
> marvelous understanding.

My thirtieth birthday, two weeks after her death. She always remembered to send a card, could never resist an opportunity to add to her collection *(let's just take a quick peek at this stationery store here . . .)*. She bought a letterpress with her fiancé and they dreamed up logos for his homebrewed beer, save-the-dates and invitations for their wedding, a new line of greeting cards. Burrowed in her handbag, a stack for any occasion—birthday, thank you, miss you, congratulations, blank—as if she might need to dispatch one at any moment. *(Contingencies.)* Among the ones that have arrived in my mailboxes over the years: Mini pouches of parsley, sage, rosemary—*let's get together if you have the thyme.* Mushrooms around a mossy boulder—*I lichens you a lot.* A grinning straight-edge gives a thumbs-up to his friend—*you rock!* and the smiling stone replies, *you rule!* A hedgehog grins at a bristle brush—*love at first sight.* The day I turn thirty, driving along a forest-encircled stretch of freeway, I am thinking there will never be another birthday card from her when I look skyward and see a rainbow painted between the clouds.

The month before she dies, GVHD has turned her stomach into a *cisuo*, needling cells rushing her repeatedly to the *cesuo*, whose sliding door is drawn when the rainbow emerges. *Wait, wait,* I plead. It does. Holds on just long enough for her to glimpse the stripes of color dissolving back into mist. Rainbows reappear the next afternoon, and the next. They are like her life: fleeting, everywhere, not conjurable by force of will, a gift, bonus.

UNDER THE DOUBLE RAINBOW AT Howth summit, salty tears mingling with ocean mist, I follow the cliff edge to a steep path, teeter down slippery stone steps onto a small beach. Bobbing heads in the water—a group of watchful seals—outnumber the smattering of people on shore.

The weather alternates between sun and rain, wind and calm, searing and freezing, stormy and fair. I prop up my flimsy umbrella, only to have it inverted by a strong gust; redome the steel-ribbed parabola, only to discover it's no longer needed; take off my down vest, shed the sweater too, so that I'm reduced to wearing a tank top, but just as I dig out my sunscreen the warm rays are gone, the icy wind back—and on it goes.

I stumble through the fickle seasons. At the end of the beach, a semblance of a cove, more or less protected from prying eyes. From the drawstring pouch that's meant to hold my down vest, I remove the hummingbird container.

Here we are, at the edge of the sea, in the country that raised a marathon runner who would teach us principles and practices for the care of the dying.

IRELAND—ALWAYS WANTED TO GO THERE!

Here we are, love, here we are.

A promise kept. A vow fulfilled. A final wish to carry through.

THE TIDE RUSHES IN—NO DAWDLING NOW!

The Atlantic laps at my shoes sprays my hair wets my jeans ferries her away on rafts of seafoam—

I am talking to airborne oceanswallowed ashes bumbling prayer suddenly laughing *alive* thankful metta-flooded

No time to linger—the water encroaches, the beach narrows, sunset looms. I clamber up the slippery stony steps, turn back to face the ocean below. A seal holds my gaze.

Then, from where I've just strewn her ashes, a rainbow emerges, bright as the one in Tibet, paving a bridge between ocean and sky.

Accidents of nature in a rainbow-prone country? Perhaps, but when I reach the bottom of the gently sloping lane that leads to Howth town and see yet another, fainter, rainbow, I think: I have not walked this path alone.

I got my sign, many times over.

A LETTER TO T:

You said there would come a flood of tears. I hear its rush now. It gathers momentum in the rivulets that streak our faces at this Portland hospital.

You will not be surprised to hear they don't think she has much time left. Though yesterday, in the precious hour that our sunrise friend and her brother's best friend and I gathered around her hospital bed, she was, as ever, 100% present. Asking about our lives. So fully and completely herself it was easy to forget that the immune cells in her body are no longer hers, the button she surreptitiously presses during our visit dispenses powerful pain meds, the bags hanging above her bed can only keep death at bay for a few hours more.

Our sunrise friend says: "life is strange." Life is strange, its fortitude and fragility, its interplay with time elastic and brittle. Here on the 14th floor oncology unit with all its love and liminality. How is it that she is so full of life and so close to death?

Even in these hard times, there is room for humor. The macabre truth oddly soothes. Her husband, in his own treeful way, says the leukemia is spreading so quickly that if you put an ear up to her you can hear it grow.

It is as you once sang. "I will say that I want it all: the joy, the pain, the tears, the laughter."

HE WRITES BACK:

How whole you are, how huge your love, in the pith of grief.

You love her with the whole of the world's love, with the enormity of everyone she has illuminated with her crystalline kindness and otherworldly grace.

You mourn her with the whole of the world's embrace, with the tears of everyone who feel hollowed by this loss, this slipping away from heartbeats, this ever-flowing cascade of love.

Your love for her honors the very best of human possibilities. Your mourning contemplates that wound from which all blood and love in this world flows.

May her memory be ever at your breath, ever in your step, ever in the skillful honing of your words. Your hearts, so vast in their openings for the raw clefts of life, deserve each other. Your infinite smiles too.

I breathe these breaths with you, with all of her family and friends. I stand here under the fragile clouds and tender raindrops, each one so hesitant to fall, bearing witness.

May you be happy. May you be well. May your grief encompass all. May your embrace be full of love.

Wishing you peace, always,

WE ARE ON A MISSION.[*] How is it that marijuana is easier to find in this city than a blueberry muffin?

I suppose it doesn't help that this is the season for pumpkins and not the season of her favorite tart-sweet fruit.

L is a Bay Area–based environmental lawyer who is exactly the type of person we need to protect our earth. You do not want to mess with this woman. L calls several bakeries in rapid succession, irritation mounting, until she finally finds one that has what we want. She makes a beeline for it, mancuvering the rental car to a screeching halt in a parking lot with no empty spaces, barks at us three whiplashed passengers to run out, *go, dudes, go!*

We tell the tattooed staff of the cinnamon-scented shop that our friend just called. They assure us with frightened expressions that they received the communiqué and point to the sparsely populated display case. The specimen they've singled out leaves us dubious. We can barely see the blueberries for the pecans/streusel/lemon/cardamom/sour-cream swirls or whatever other nonsense they paired (trioed? quinteted?) them with. L rushes in, keys jangling. She assesses the situation. She is not amused. The staff are ready to wilt into the croissants.

Back on the phone again. We have become a flock of xenophobic harpies. No! None of that weird stuff, just a PLAIN GODDAMN BLUEBERRY MUFFIN. *Not* boysenberry, NOT sour cream—are you kidding me?! What do we have to do to find a NORMAL f***-ing blueberry muffin in this town?!

Just as we are beginning to wonder if it might be faster to break into someone's kitchen and bake a batch ourselves—

We find what we're looking for. Oh, joyous day!

And oh, more joyous still, watching her eat that muffin with relish, the way I've seen her eat countless others, long fingernails making short shrift of the blueberries. It's a monumental feat. A quarter of that mammoth muffin gone in a single sitting, round boulder transfigured to pockmarked cove. The most sweet-faced and foul-mouthed of her middle school friends will recall at the

---

[*] We being her brother, his best friend L, our sunrise friend, and me

memorial—in mock exasperation and loving jest—*Why did she have to mangle every baked good instead of just taking bites like a normal person?!* (Only she says it with more expletives.)

I knew it would be the last thing she ever ate.

Her wishes: always an adventure, never a burden.

I ARRIVE IN DOWNTOWN HOWTH a half hour before sunset, too early for dinner, too dazed to find my way back to Dublin.

An Irishman falls in step beside me. He too is out for a stroll, "on the doss" as he calls it. Bald head a shade lighter than his beige trench coat, expression unreadable behind black sunglasses. It's the cut of his coat that makes my blood run cold.

"Don't underestimate the trauma," a teacher of chaplaincy and Zen had warned me in the immediate aftermath, when there were still police reports and court orders to file. Of the handful of people I confided in, nearly all the women could relate, some with stories far more harrowing. How long the tail of fear, how lancing the tower of guilt. I remember that howling evening at the hospital. *It won't be finished in a day.*

The tail is barbed and prone to lashing me just when I think it has gone dormant for good. The tower is jerry-built and evades my attempts to escape its crush. I thought I would be free of them in Ireland, but no. I am stung into paralysis, pelted and trapped. I shouldn't fear this stranger, surely he means me no harm, my instincts say he can be trusted. But instinct once betrayed me badly, and that is the most poisoned arrow of all, that I no longer trust my own intuition.

BUT MY FRIEND WHOSE ASHES I have just scattered would tell me, *This armor of mistrust does not become you either.* And all the crying has me feeling vulnerable and flayed. Alive but tender.

Chitchat for the first few minutes. He is an affable enough walking companion through the safe territory of small talk.

"Would you like a cup of tea?" I surprise myself by nodding. The wind sharpens its bite as sunset approaches; a hot drink would be nice, though it's too late in the day for caffeine. The nearest shop doesn't have anything decaf, so we try again farther down the street.

"A cup of herbal tea for the lady, please." Though far from impeccably dressed, this stranger reminds me of the mayor at the hospital with his easy rapport and unassuming kindness. The two drinks don't cost much. He fishes a crumpled five-euro note from his coat pocket, insists on paying for both. We nurse the paper cups by the harbor. He's glad it's not dawn, when the seals make a frightful noise—and stench—as they vie for the discarded innards of the early morning catch.

The Irishman remains an enigma. "I'm not wealthy, but I don't work very much," he tells me. I shiver, cradling the cup of now-lukewarm chamomile. I wish I'd chosen to stay in the café. The few passersby are wisely bundled up in windbreakers. At least my conversation partner has taken off the sunglasses. His eyes are bluish-gray, his face lined.

"If you don't mind me asking, what brings you here?"

I am guarded, but I am also a bad liar. Sometimes simplicity is best. "I came here to scatter a dear friend's ashes. We always wanted to visit Ireland together."

He doesn't say he's sorry.

"You did a powerful and important thing. Your whole day has had the quality of ritual."

He pauses.

"But it is a sad day too."

ON ONE OF MY FIRST visits as a volunteer chaplain, I meet a Lebanese Catholic woman in her sixties with tousled gray hair. She dabs at her younger sister's parched lips with a moistened sponge. The sister, eyes shut behind plastic rims, wears a pinkish-lavender sweater and carefully applied—not by her own hand—lipstick and blush to match.

I marvel at the older woman's care.

She smiles. "People ask me, *how can you be so patient?* I say, how can you not? My sister is a saint. I would stay here all night if they let me. She has sepsis now, which is what our mom died of a year ago. My sister has schizophrenia and she thinks Mom is still alive. I haven't the heart to tell her otherwise, so I tell her, when you're better, we can see her together."

Her concern overflows to encompass me. "You're so young to be a chaplain. It must be difficult work. Do you come from a happy, stable family? Did you have an easy time growing up?"

I say what I think she wants to hear—*yes*—though this is at best a partial truth, then pose the same questions back to her. She tells me about their alcoholic father. The brother who loves them very much but doesn't understand mental illness. The other residents of the skilled nursing facility where her sister usually lives—they are kindred too, she just bought a radio for one of them.

"I can't remember a time when I didn't feel burdened." I expect bitterness in her voice but find none. "Some people ask, *why me*, but I say, *why not me?*" At home, the room where her sister once lived has remained untouched since the day she left for the facility, when the illness became too much for them to manage at home.

Sometimes all you have to do is name what you taste on the tip of your tongue. "There is sadness in that room . . ." I venture.

She starts to cry. "It's so hard, sometimes I fantasize about taking my sister home, but I can't."

We part with a short prayer and a warm embrace. A schizophrenic saint and her lifelong devotee: unable to fix anything, caring for each other still.

"You need to cry."

The Irishman, named for the patron saint of pregnant women, was simply naming what he saw.

He is right, of course, but even chaplains don't always want to face the truth.

His last name is Polish. He is, like me, the child of immigrants. Like me, an only child. *Us sibling-less children are high achievers,* he theorizes. *It's because we only have ourselves to compete with.* That, he implies, makes it harder for us to grieve.

Perhaps so. There is some notion of the right way to mourn (five stages, anyone?), no small shame in the label of *complicated grief* in a culture so fixated on moving on, ever onwards to the better beyond.

I am trying not to cry in front of this complete stranger. Even though at the hospital, so many people cried in front of me, a complete stranger.

He's right, the tears are still close, threatening to spill forth at the slightest provocation, the seals their only witnesses today. I'm scared. Wanting to trust, but scared.

I am beginning to sense that this is no ordinary stranger. He asks, respectfully, *May I place a palm on your face, like this?* He demonstrates on his own scruffy cheek. *Here above your neck, just for a moment?* He is asking to release my tears. I refuse. He nods in understanding but doesn't apologize for the odd request. He knows as well as I that this is not a titillating story about a creepy old man.

That wound—her death. She who was better than a sister to me, my familiar. And that other wound, the one that makes me panic upon glancing a certain cut of coat or a particular model of car, that tells me nobody in this world can be trusted.

MY CURIOSITY GETS THE BETTER of me. I ask the stranger to tell me more about himself.

He does tai chi, swims in the icy sea (it's an Irish thing), jogs, has a heart that has stopped three times.

My heart skips a beat. "You said you don't work much, but—what exactly is it that you do?"

"I do Reiki. Have you heard of it?"

一期一會. I CAN ONLY NOD, dumbfounded.*

My college roommate would discover Reiki independently of me. I first received Reiki in South Africa; she in California. I would go on to learn it in Phnom Penh; she in Oregon.

Rev. B had gone to Cambodia to teach indigent AIDS patients how to meditate. She quickly realized they could barely afford medicine and food; how would they muster up the energy to hold lotus poses for hours on end? So, she changed tack. Learned Reiki and taught this type of energy healing to Brahmavihara's Cambodian staff, many of whom were themselves HIV-positive. Their patients don't care to debate the origins or efficacy of the technique, which was developed by a Japanese Buddhist in the 1920s. They simply love to receive it. They call it a meditation of the hands. A meditation that soothes in a different way than the medicine and food the Brahmavihara staff also bring.

The summer after I graduate from college, Rev. B and her staff teach me Reiki. This is how it feels to be humbled. My newly minted college degree is utterly useless for alleviating the suffering of the Cambodians who await death in ailing hospitals and threadbare jails. Not knowing Khmer, I can offer little more than my presence and a meditation of my hands. It is world-altering to discover that this can be enough. Just this much: enough. For an incurable perfectionist, an inveterate striver, that summer is myth-shattering.†

---

* Of all the things in the world he could be, a farmer, an actuary, a truck driver, an elementary school teacher . . .

† The American dream, the bootstraps, etc. etc.

THE REIKI PRACTITIONER IS REVEALED. The rest is a foregone conclusion. I allow him to place his hand against my cheek. I close my eyes. I heave with sobs.

Chaplains need chaplains too.

HE HAS REACHED BEYOND MY papered-on smiles to the torrent of sorrow.

"It's good to wash the eyes every once in a while, with one's own tears."

Sometimes, chaplains offer not prayer or scripture, but plain old common sense.

"It's ok to feel depleted. All this travel takes a toll on the body."

Suddenly I feel heavy as the sand-barges that plunder the riverbed of the Mekong. All those mornings in Phnom Penh, I ran past evidence of that ruinous appetite for construction.

"If a boy gets a gash on his arm that requires stitches, how would you care for it?"

Tenderly?

"Yes, by cleaning and dressing it daily. You wouldn't take a cheese grater to it!"

I laugh, though I know what it's like to grate my wounds, year in and year out. How hard it is to let them be.

"You can't fix it—but you can let it heal."

The terrains of grief, the wilds of loss—I have not navigated them alone in these ocean-traversing years.

The Reiki man smiles. "Now, who says it's too cold for ice cream?"

"YOU CAN'T COME TO IRELAND without having a 99!" The young man who makes my cone was born and raised in Howth. He dispenses the vanilla soft serve with the precision of a lapidary.

"Flake?" I nod. "Good! Without the Flake it's not a 99, it's just ice cream." He inserts the chocolate-covered wafer with reverential concentration, then admires the finished product.

We make sloppy mess of the artisan's serious(ly melting) handiwork. I have ice cream all over my nose.

Classic chaplaincy: Pause here. Sit awhile. Go on, what else? Heart cry. Belly laugh. The truth of all encounters: We might never meet again. 沧海一鳞, a scale in the sea.

Classic confidentiality: I won't speak of this again unless you bring it up. 沧海桑田, the oceans transform to mulberry fields.

I accept a ride back to Dublin. He finds his way without the intervention of GPS. We haven't touched a phone this entire time. His lilting patter is our radio. The landscapes of his adopted home country come alive through his stories. *You must go to Kerry; it's timeless.*

Perhaps generosity doesn't play by the usual idioms, an eye for an eye, tit for tat, you scratch my back and I'll scratch yours. Still, I ask him point blank: *What's in this for you?* Distraction from pain. He'd been in a car accident, hit by a truck, and wasn't seeing his chiropractor until later this week. What I don't tell him: *I once knew a man who wore an olive-green trench coat; he rolled down a ravine in his car and survived, though for some of us the outcome is the same, he is a haunting ghost.*

Inversion: the color of the coat, the model of the car, the arrangement of the steering wheel. The alleviation and not genesis of suffering.

A parting story: At the airport, a man says to his daughter, "I wish you enough." She begins to cry, *but you've always given me more than enough,* walks away bawling. An onlooker asks, apologetic: *I couldn't help but notice . . .* The father replies, "Oh yes, it may be the last time we see each other. We live far apart. I have a life-limiting illness." *I'm so sorry,* the stranger stammers. "No, no, it's no problem."

Closing blessings: I wish you enough rain to appreciate the sunshine, enough cold to appreciate the warmth, enough hunger to appreciate your fullness—and enough sadness to cherish your happiness. I wish you enough. You will be ok.

Love,

I was so happy and so sad today. It was the type of day you never forget. A once-in-a-lifetime day. (Though isn't that true of every day?)

The Reiki bodhisattva asked many questions I couldn't answer.

Why so much travel? Sometimes one's tank is empty, he murmurs, almost to himself. (Yes, the travel is wearing, but I can't seem to prevent a new country's stamp from appearing on my passport every two months. Sometimes one's grief bank is full.)

Do you believe in reincarnation? (The moment we first met in this lifetime, I felt I had known you before, what an unbelievable gift to meet again. I had been searching for home for so, so long. You listened me home.)

I told him I cried when I saw the double rainbow. He said only, "good."

He had to reassure me: I won't hurt you. I had to believe him. His touch was warm and cold, firm and soft, yellow light behind my closed eyelids, sure and kind, present without exploiting or demanding or extracting. He was cautious: I don't want to intrude on your relationship with her. A fine line, witness and healer, possessor and controller. An ambiguous ability, to see into people as this man with his thrice-halted heart and the shamaness who is your name-twin are able to do.

Ground your feet. Take a hot bath. Watch the water drain, every last drop. I follow these instructions until the tub has emptied of all but a few speckles of silt. Shiver no more. Exhausted dreamless sleep.

DEAREST,

You would love the handmade card I saw at a coffee shop on my final day in Ireland, perfect for the parents of our soon-to-be-born niece. Not the obvious stork in the sky with swaddled babe dangling from its beak, but a fat white bird captioned "It's a gull!" That most ubiquitous of beach birds, filcher of fried foods along boardwalks everywhere. Inside the card: "Welcome little miss."

Your brother would like the Irish bros turned vegans who offer free porridge at their café every morning. I read in their cookbook: "Karma means you don't get away with anything." I would say: Karma means we have more power than we know.

The vitality of ritual. Run. Shower. Eat. Walk. Bus ride. Rain. Sun. Rainbows. Cry. Path. Sea level. Far cove. Incoming tide. Laughing scattering confetti ashes. Seals. Goodbyes. Tea. Ice cream. Spills. Smears. Soak. Sleep. Our pilgrimage to Ireland.

The last day in Ireland, rainbows bookend my walk at Greystones. Form is emptiness is . . . Dear friend, separated from me by distance and time and now emptinessform—this is still a Conversation with a capital C, to be continued . . .

AFTER THAT TRIP, THE CRYING flows easier, sudden as Irish rain. What a relief.

SOON IT WILL BE ~~TWO~~ ~~three~~ ~~four~~ ~~five~~ years. Will I still be angry, her brother numb? Someone I love died, we say, a part of us died. Will I still be OCD, devastated when I misplace my only pair of meditation-appropriate pants, overcome when I lose a fuzzy sock?

I think about Mrs. C missing her daughter. Mr. C raising an A-OK.

I give myself permission not to keep it together.

It's ok if all my life I cry beneath rainbowed skies.

PART VII: 一念三千

ichinen sanzen

THEY CALL THEMSELVES "REAL SHANGHAINESE," born and raised. Like my dad, family roots in the region burrowing back multiple generations. Unlike my mom, teased mercilessly for her Cantonese accent as a newly arrived elementary school student in pre–Cultural Revolution Shanghai.

The couple apologizes for their laughable 普通话. Few of their vintage remain; the rest are scattered around the globe. They speak to me in Shanghainese. I understand but can't speak my father tongue, so I respond in Mandarin. We apologize for our respective linguistic shortcomings, though we needn't. The conversation flows effortlessly.

She rolls her eyes at her husband's loquaciousness but can't suppress a smile. Her husband narrates the story for me. His beloved has been thrice in the hospital, thrice at death's door. They married late, in their forties. The concentration of their affection for each other is thick enough to lick the lost years. I'm reminded of the creamy layer on the soy milk my mom makes every Saturday morning, 豆腐衣 chopsticks-plucked from the well of hot 豆浆. In Old Shanghai the beverage would be smoky from burnt contact with the meter-wide vat, the mouth-melt on its surface broad enough to swallow the setting moon.

They know the street I grew up on. She says we Shanghainese are 灵.[*] Sharp, spirited, capable. Of good ilk. I let her include me in her grand *we,* suspending my caveats and exceptions. The husband tells me he loves adventure. He won't travel without his beloved, though. No matter—it's a thrill just to look at photos online. He pulls out his iPad and treats me to the Eiffel Tower, Big Ben, Taj Mahal.

None of us know that five years from now, this will become the safest way to travel, thanks to a virus that will emerge five hundred miles west of Shanghai and quickly unmoor the entire world. We will stare at photos of the places and people we desperately want to visit. Even those of us who are not hospital-bound will feel crushed by the interminable wait of an unknowable prognosis.

---

[*] The first character of Reiki 灵气, rendered rococo in traditional script as 靈氣

"YOUR OWN DISCOMFORT IS NOT a good reason to leave the room." Another of our chaplaincy adages, right up there with death ≠ emergency, the patients are our greatest teachers, anger = energy, the patients aren't here to see us.

Don't bolt. Linger awhile. I practice against habit.

Sometimes persistence turns me into a vampire, sometimes it bears sweeter fruit. One patient rebuffs my first visit. I decide, cautiously, to check in once more. He invites me in, apologizing for his previous rudeness. Every day is different. A "bad visit" today does not guarantee the same tomorrow; so too with the "good" visits, which are capricious as the worldly winds of praise and blame, pleasure and pain, fame and shame, loss and gain. The chaplain as exegete of living human documents soon realizes her texts are ever-shifting palimpsests in a Babelian library of open books and locked diaries.

I meet a patient who's pissed off. I manage to make some leeway until I mention his doctor. *Now YOU'RE irritating me,* the man snarls. *Get out!* I go back the next day: *I don't want to talk right now.* I go back the next day. His expression is contrite. *Hey chaplain, my spirits are higher.* He confesses that his brothers and sister-in-law gave him a talking to; it was her tough love that broke through his blustering. *I'm scared,* he admits. He gives me a big hug when I leave. *Thank you so much. Thank you for everything.* Let the glory go to God, and his sister in law too.

My initial interpretations are often wrong. My second and third impressions too. When I first meet Mr. S, he is gruff and dismissive. "Declined chaplain visit," I dutifully chart. He stays at the hospital longer than expected; I hazard another visit. Again he is guarded, brushes me off with an *everything's fine.* I have added a column to the census of people on my units to help me prioritize who to see: length of stay. His LOS drifts into double digits. His religion column reads "Baptist."

When Mr. S transfers to a different room, I poke my head in to see how he's doing. "You moved," I remark. "Sometimes people feel a little more isolated in this corner."

"Come on in," he replies, baritone voice gravelly. "Sit."

Maya Angelou was right. I no longer remember what was said and done, but I remember the feeling of that afternoon and the ones thereafter. We spend much of our time in companionable silence. I have become endeared of this Baptist gentleman's reticence, the way he murmurs, *you come by again, okay?* at the end of every visit.

There's only one entrance to every patient's room, but so many ways to drop into a conversation. Sleepwalker moments strike often: what path did I take to get here? Snuck in through a side door, squeezed in through the cat door. This stealth is not for thievery, though the quiet pauses between our breaths feel like stolen moments of defiant restoration.

My first taste of flying, at an ice-skating rink in Pittsburgh. A stranger grabs my hand and takes me for a spin. The ice loses its frigidity, my wobbly legs embolden, the slippery pond transforms to open sky. Ephemeral but solid, strange but safe, fleeting but trustworthy, these bodhisattvas in different guises.

We may never know what we mean to others, and vice versa.

In all our visits, I saw the Baptist man cry just once, when he told me about a woman who came to pray for him. It was the simplest of benedictions. *May God steady the hand of the surgeon.*

THE MUTED PAST, OUR MUZZLED HISTORIES. Two decades after the fact, I learn that my mother started a memoir once. Like my half-uncle's probable murder, my great-grandmother's Buddhist chants, my never-would-be sibling's capitulation to the one-child policy, she mentions the fragment of memoir offhand, belatedly. When I ask her about it, my mother texts back: "I remember I titled it 14 bd for your 14th birthday. It was meant to be your birthday present but never finished, not even close."

Looking for the file, she finds something else written on my behalf that also never reached its target audience. LetterToLowerProjectLoad.doc begins with a reflection on the types of assignments required for our "highly capable classes" (not the official name for my International Baccalaureate program). "The students were required to do many projects, most of the projects were somewhat related to artistic design: making posters, binding books, designing games, and even making stuffed animals." I still have my laboriously drawn map of Washington State, the denim wildebeest that robbed me of a night's sleep and a pair of jeans.

My mom goes on to complain, "To a student who is not a quick artist, these projects took a tremendous amount of time to complete. My child spent more time drawing, cutting, and pasting than actually writing and studying, and usually stayed up past 12 a.m. for a few days before the project was due." She proposes reducing the number of these types of projects, or at least lowering their artistic standards. "I would rather see a healthy and happy child instead of a stressed-out child struggling to cut and paste one poster after another." She points out that stress and sleep deprivation can lead to poor mental and physical health as well as substance abuse.

In conclusion: "It seems that the 21st century children must stay up well past midnight: partying, using drugs, or doing school projects. Is there a time machine for us to go back to the dinosaur age when children finished homework at 8 p.m. and went to bed before 10 p.m.?"

I read these paragraphs and sense the futility of calculating what's owed. This woman I warred with so many years—funny how I didn't know her at all. How I still, in countless ways, don't.

I WORRY THAT MR. S will go the way of Mr. X, languishing in the hospital until his demise. It's been months since Mr. S has been able to eat. His nutrition comes in liquid forum, via PEG tube. Sometimes his nurse comes in during our visits to hang a new bag.

And then comes the day Mr. S is finally allowed to eat what he has been requesting for weeks. When it arrives, I recognize the treat from summer camps past: the disposable cup, the infinity-shaped wood spoon. Mr. S eats the orange sherbet like it's been served on a silver platter. The years melt from his face, horsepower in reverse: sixty to six in one tiny, glorious lick. He is glowing. I must be too. The sheer joy of it!

That sherbet is as good as shared—like those ice cream bars with polar bears on the wrapper that I used to eat with my dad, squares imperfectly bisected along the diagonal with a spoon. We would crack the coating like crème brûlée, embedding shards of chocolate into the vanilla core.

I was wrong to say I never ate with such gusto again after the fried chicken that first week in America. Watching a recovering patient relish the most sublime of orange sherbets, witnessing a dying friend savor her very last blueberry muffin, I learn there's another way to eat with my whole being, a way where the food never even touches my tongue.

Outside the hospital walls, it is spring. Inside, the seasonless room has become summertime, a porch in the South, a 阳台 in Shanghai, a meditation hall in Cambodia after a ten-day silent retreat where Rev. B is saying, with pleasure, to me and the Brahmavihara staff, *now your feet are on the path.*

That time machine, it does exist.

IN MY NIGHTMARE, SHE DIES. I wake up sobbing. The Buddhist fiancé responds with the gentleness of a mule deer: "She can't die twice." I'm comforted by this fact. To die again and again would be hell, not just for the dying but those of us still living.

A few months later T and I go for a bike ride. Pedaling up the steepest hill with Mount Diablo in the distance, he jokes we've reached the peak of Mount Sumeru. Huffing and sweat-drenched, I ask, *So does that mean we can die happy now?* "Nah, let's stay in the human realm a bit longer." *Keep cycling through samsara together then?* "That'd be a good name for a Buddhist biking group, Cycling Through Samsara."

Going on living means piling up these silly moments. It gives me pause when I watch a new movie in the theaters and realize it's full of references she'll never hear. I want to tell her about a scene at the feisty main character's Catholic high school. "Remember that you are dust," the priest intones, "and to dust you shall return." He smudges the students' foreheads. This honest declaration of mortality strikes me as thoroughly Buddhist, though maybe that's just me apprehending the world through Dharma-tinted lenses. If I were that priest, I might find Catholicism in Buddhist holidays.

I was on call Ash Wednesday of my CPE year. Our Catholic priest was off, so it fell to me to fulfill the request of a group of radiation technicians to mark the beginning of Lent.

One of our supervisors, a Catholic laywoman, gives me the ashes. I fret over my lack of authority, my liturgical illiteracy on this holy day. As would appear to be the case with the overwhelming majority of my worries, no one else is the least worked up. No one chastises my collarless neck. Everyone, even the non-Christians, wants to wear a trace of gray. And why not? Without these marks, how are we to give shape to the soup of our days? Non-Christian that I am, I do not command them to repent and believe in the Gospel, but I wish for each RT peace and healing and renewal. I pray they will be smudged by love on this and all of their days.

NEWLY ARRIVED IN A SUBURB of Seattle, my mom took me to a Unitarian Universalist church on Sundays. It was a noble attempt to remedy my friendless state. Alas, the visits only exacerbated my social anxiety. I couldn't stop noticing how we were the only non-white people in the entire congregation.

Newly arrived in a suburb of Seattle, living 2,500 miles away from her husband and daughter, in the months before her only child came to live with her, my mom visited a Catholic church for a time. Until she told me this, I'd thought my mother impervious to the lure of religious community. It was confession that did her in. The relentless pace at which sins had to be exhumed! She started making them up.

In the fragment of memoir she didn't give me on my fourteenth birthday, Mom writes about a more successful conversion.

I was born prematurely, only weighed 5.5 lb. I was called "thermostat" because I was so little (maybe also fragile). My parents and grandmother tried to feed me everything considered nutritious for babies at that time: all kinds of bird eggs and animal livers . . . My younger sister was born in 1961. My mother was given the ration to buy some eggs. So my parents built a small incubator trying to convert the eggs into chickens.

The converts themselves weren't particularly memorable.

I don't remember those chickens, but there was one rooster who became our family legend, because he ate too much and stuffed his gut hard as a stone. My mother had to perform a small operation on him—cutting his gut to get the excess food out.

The interventions of my mother's mother, nurse-turned-veterinarian for the day, couldn't cure the rooster's cravings.

When he was stitched back, he was picking up the food on the operation table—a typical hungry creature in that period. It is a common belief in China that people born in that period of time are always hungry in the rest of their live. This may explain my husband's good appetites because he was born in 1959. My younger sister had the same reputation when she was little.

At a temple in Chiangmai, my parents and I puzzle over a framed photograph of a regal-looking rooster. The accompanying Thai text explains that this feathered temple-goer has been the most devout of worshippers. He pecked at anyone who forgot to remove their shoes or failed to pay respect to the Buddha. I can't help but press my palms together and ไหว้ to the portrait of the fearsome fowl.

GUANGZHOU. BEIJING. DALIAN. MY MOTHER moved three times in the first three years of her life. "I must be a very forgetful person," she writes—yet she retains a memory from 北京:

We lived in a SiHeYuan—a type of old housing structure very typical in Bei-Jing. The structure had four houses built to form a shared square or rectangular common area called "TianJing" (sky well), where neighbors would socialize in the evenings. The place had a strange name "NiuQuan" (cow stable), so we were all cows for two years. It was torn down when we left there. The only impression I had for that place was the day we were moving out, there was this giant date tree cut down and lying in the "TianJing", and my grandmother and I were picking up dates and eating them while waiting for the moving truck.

不要问我从哪里来	Do not ask me where I come from
我的故乡在远方	My hometown is far away
为什么流浪	Why do I wander?
流浪远方	Wander afar
流浪	Wandering
为了天空飞翔的小鸟	For the birds that soar in the sky
为了山间轻流的小溪	For the brooks that flow in the hills
为了宽阔的草原	For the vast grasslands
流浪远方	Wandering afar
流浪	Wandering
还有还有	And too, and too,
为了梦中的枣子树	For my dreamed date tree
枣子树	Date tree

THE YOUNGER SISTER WHO WOULD go on to read dictionaries cover to cover during the Cultural Revolution was born in Dalian. Of this port city in northeastern China, my mother writes:

I have a little more memory for DaLian than for Beijing, but not much more. We lived in an apartment building. There was a beach not far away, where my grandmother and I went quite often to pick up seaweeds. We were in DaLian from 1958 to 1961, when the famine period called "three-year natural disaster" was coming. So anything edible was not wasted, including seaweeds. I went to a day care center. Everyday I was given two potatoes plus salt for lunch. My family was a little better off than most of the families, because my father had some kind of coupons allowing him to buy some rice and eggs. So I wasn't as hungry as other kids in my day care center. I didn't like the taste of potatoes, and was always the last one to swallow my lunch, causing a lot of blames from the teacher—a child was supposed to finish his/her lunch as quickly as possible. This dislike of potatoes lasted half of my life until I came to the States, where potatoes taste slightly different and more tolerable, especially when cooked as French fries and potato chips.

I find out that her grandmother was Buddhist when my mom is fifty-three and I am twenty-five. At a diasporic Chinese temple in San Francisco, I bite into a delicious tuber that is crunchy on the outside and starchy on the inside. I email a photo to Mom, who identifies it as 慈姑. *It's available around this Chinese New Year season. My grandma and I used to cut it very thin and deep-fry it like a potato chip.* When I point out that 慈 is a core tenet of the religion I came to adopt in America, she reveals my great-grandmother's penchant for Cantonese Buddhist chants. Those chants would be even more indecipherable to me than they were for my mother, who at least knows Cantonese. And yet part of me believes there would be no impediment to understanding her, none at all.

WHEN I ASK MY MOM about her forays into Catholicism, she tells me I've mixed up my memories. It wasn't a Catholic confession, but a group of people at a Chinese church, "holding hands and talking about the sins."

What we say and how we're interpreted will always be two separate things, won't they? Mom's unfinished memoir opens with these lines:

My mother kept a diary for me, in which she recorded many details in my early life. I only have a very few memory of my childhood before 6, so my mother's diary together with words from relatives and friends provided the missing link connecting me to this world.

The history of China in the 20th century is a complicated mixture of war and class struggle—people fight against people even in peaceful time. I have not the slightest interest in learning the history, one reason being there are so many versions of the history from different parties, that none would agree on what really happened. Therefore, whatever I will describe here were from my point of view, which was influenced by my family, relatives and friends, and may not be the reality as viewed by others.

Caveat emptor. Like mother, like daughter. This memoir is only one imperfect chaplain's view of reality.

A MAN WITH A RARE and incurable neurological condition has just reread Camus's *The Myth of Sisyphus.* He's not sure if it's worth pushing anymore.

When I start burning out during my CPE residency, it feels like rolling a boulder up the mountain, only to be daily flattened. I don't mention this to him; I'm wary of false equivalences. It's tempting to downplay my privileges and power for fear of abusing them, but there is no denying this most obvious of differences: though I spend my days in the kingdom of the sick, I always retire to the queendom of the well. I am daily in cancer's proximity but have never been its bearer.

I assess whether he is suicidal. No, but a little tired at the edges of life.

"I am not where I expected to be," he sighs. Nor I, fellow traveler, nor I.

He sees the end of the tunnel clearer now that he is sixty-six and not six. "I don't have much time left." His work has been as a ghostwriter, unacknowledged.

"I like you, you make me feel very comfortable and at ease," he tells me. I marvel that though he can no longer trust his body to do his bidding, his trust in others is wholly intact, a guileless gift.

He has a sibling eight years his junior. Even before she was born, he would speak to her with uncontainable excitement: "Sister, sister, when are you coming out?" He presents me a gleaming memory of a stolen day they once spent together at Central Park.

After the listening, the blessing is easier. I pray for his yearnings. Ease with not knowing. Magic of unfettered days.

Two years later, a dear friend will write, "Remember—the difficult moments (amazingly) do not last forever. Seek solace in knowing they too shall pass."

A few weeks before she dies, this entry: "I hear a lot of words like 'unfair' or 'sorry.' But if you think about it, aren't these all just bonus years? Am I not just extraordinarily lucky? In this moment, sipping coffee and watching dawn paint downtown Portland in pastels, there is nowhere else I'd rather be."

STORIES WANDER AROUND THE HOSPITAL, seeking to be cochlea-heard, atria-housed. Some days, there is nowhere else I'd rather be, nothing else I'd rather do. My heart is a capacious hotel for any caprices that come its way. For the man who doesn't want to leave, first upsetting his breakfast onto the floor, then pretending to sleep—deceptions born of desperation, as he has no home to go to. For the coup de grâce of ashes—his grandma, rumor has it. After the code gray and before the cleanup, the room is a modern art exhibit, aglitter in stardust.

LANDING IN SAN FRANCISCO IN early March of 2020, we expect to head back to Thailand the following month. *Hey,* our closest friend in Bangkok texts. *I think you're either just about arriving in the States or already there; hope the journey went smoothly. I've been seeing a number of news articles lately about coronavirus-related racism against Asians in the US so be sure to stay safe . . . both from the virus and the racism!*

W's message isn't the only reason this visit feels uncanny. There's the cavalier attitude toward mask-wearing at the airport. The officer who waves us through with unnerving swiftness, before we have a chance to explain our recent trips to China and Nepal, Taiwan and Laos.

Newly pregnant, my friend who is named for sunrise cancels our nine-months-in-the-making plans to meet up. She grew up in Hong Kong; a close family friend was one of the first people in the world to die of SARS. Her Bay Area coworkers wonder if she's overreacting. In retrospect, they should have taken her lead. In retrospect, I shouldn't have been shocked when our month-long visit to the Bay turned into an indefinite stay.

Living eight thousand miles away, I'd missed our ten-year college reunion the previous autumn. My attendance at previous reunions—university, high school, or otherwise—has been precisely zero, but I'd seriously considered flying back to open the time capsule a small group of us had been saving for the decade-marking occasion. Among the treasures in the capsule was a letter from a dormmate who died in 2016.

Unbidden, my sunrise friend texts a photo of the letter to me a few hours after I land at SFO. When I start to read the words on my phone screen, it's not jetlag that makes my legs give out.

For the first time, I feel like I am letting myself feel the weight of a major life change as it is happening . . .

What will these next years bring?

How will I do in life?

My health?

My friends' health?

It's a letter to herself, but it's also a letter to all of us. On the bottom third of that single sheet of lined notebook paper, each of us gets a line, our names followed by a string of qualities: honesty, caring, vigor, sincerity, dedication. And then, the last line.

Me: scared, loving, sad, grateful.

I read in that whisper of a word, *me,* the collective voice of a world in limbo she isn't here to witness.

After her sisters died, she washed her hands often enough to earn an OCD diagnosis. Now the whole world rubs their hands raw, all of our grief banks are full, we are avalanched in a surfeit of sorrow, so many of us are numb.

Sometimes, it feels like she just died today, the grief is that fresh. Does time really heal everything?

Slumped against the wall, I allow myself to be racked by sobs. I let myself grieve.

This is just the beginning.

KARMA IS LIKE THAT RIVER in Taiwan, the silver fish constantly turning.

The river is four stories below our feet. We stand on a strip of metal grate two hundred meters long. The cargo net sways with every lurching step across the single-lane rope bridge.

Set in a lushly forested canyon, the hundred-meter-wide river we're traversing is shallow and clear. Even from this heart-stopping height, I can see the schools of silver fish that wink at us with their whole bodies. They sparkle and dull, sparkle and dull, mirroring and trapping the light in unceasing alternation.

The Buddhist hubby flies over the sequined river, elated by our soaring heights. I stagger across in mesmerized terror, hoping we won't plummet to instant death among the firefly fish.

Back in Bangkok after our visa run to Taiwan, we discover a full-grown dove on our fifteenth-floor balcony. It has no visible injuries, but it's clearly unwell, hobbling around in shock. I'm transported back to a quarter century ago, the baby red robin fallen from its nest. Prohibited from touching it, forbidden from bringing it home, I considered never leaving. Even then, I must have had faith that my witnessing, my accompaniment, could matter in some infinitesimal way, even—or especially—when there was nothing to be done.

But we have to leave to renew our Thai visa at immigration, the deadline is tomorrow. I can't stomach the thought of the dove baking on this barren balcony. The maintenance man deftly captures the bird and relocates it to the ground floor, transforming apartment landscaping into avian hospice.

We're heading out the door when the whir of the air purifier catches our ear. The number, usually in the teens, reads 200. Whereupon we learn that our balcony air conditioning unit is on fire.

Run to the hallway extinguisher, pull the pin, aim the nozzle up, no time to close the balcony door—an eruption of silt puts out the blaze chokes up our throats spews into every corner of our living room—

It takes twelve hours to clean up afterward.

How can we blame the dove, who must have chewed a wire while trying to build a nest in the AC unit, when its strange behavior also saved us? The apartment could have gone up in flames, we could have been put in a Thai prison had the fire spread to the neighbors.[*] After the innocent bird dies, how we cherish that apartment, cherish our freedom too.

---

[*] So the maintenance man informs us, impervious to our protestations over lack of just cause

ME: SCARED, LOVING, SAD, GRATEFUL.

The letter in the time capsule ushers in a season of daily crying. In retrospect, I will think of it as anticipatory grief—for the singular life in Bangkok we are about to lose, for the millions of lives the globe will lose, casualties of a world-upending pandemic.

I am immensely grateful for W, who manages, by no small miracle, to gain entry to our Bangkok apartment and direct the local employees of an international shipping company to set aside the landlord's furniture, pack up our essentials, donate the rest. It all happens at the eleventh hour, moments before the Thai government imposes a curfew that would have made the move impossible.

Four months later, books and clothing and a memoir-in-progress arrive totally intact. I will have cried more in those four months than over the past four years. I will think of it as anticipatory grief, and only later will I permit it to be more than forward-looking. Déjà vu: the feeling of being foreign and feared, irrevocably lost, unable to find my way home. Waving *zaijian* to a life that only hindsight knows is permanently foreclosed.

It's commemoratory grief as well.

There is a Cambodian belief that each of us have nineteen *proleung;* in Thailand, it's thirty-two *khwan.* I don't know how to translate ប្រលឹង or ขวัญ, whose denotation is simultaneously plural and singular. Souls, perhaps. However we designate them, they have a tendency to startle easily, stray wantonly. There are rituals to bind these astral spirits to the body, to call them back when they have wandered off. I wonder if any of mine stayed behind on the ซอย of Bangkok, the Champs-Élysées of Phnom Penh, the 弄堂 of Shanghai. I wonder, if we can't sing our lost souls home, how they might be lullabied to rest.

MY SUNRISE FRIEND IS SEVEN months pregnant when we decide to spend a masked afternoon hiking one of our favorite trails. Grassland ridge is about to give way to redwood forest when a rattlesnake's warning sunders the air. Adrenaline and instinct—I grip her arm and pull hard, away from the giant serpent, who is close enough to strike and hit flesh.

Then I apologize profusely for violating covid precautions. She's the first person I've touched all year besides the Buddhist hubby. My sunrise friend says in this case, it's ok we failed to stay six feet apart.

Covid is that snake, fangs bared, tail rattling. The highest office in the nation tells us it's just a piece of twine. I want to bite in rage. I remember how the gaslighting feels, how it de-souled* me.

The hubby is applying for academic jobs and what comes out in his otherwise unsentimental cover letters is: *Death's shadow poisons the air.*

The children, they feel it. One boy dutifully hands his toys over to his puzzled mother. "What for?" she asks. "Disinfection," he responds soberly. Another boy, confined to a stroller, loses it when an older kid on a bike whizzes past. "I'm going to get the virus!" the eighteen-month-old wails.

---

* de-soulsed?

I ADMIRE THAT WAILING KID. The real heartbreak is the adults who want to cry but can't. I understand, the way pain hardens us. After a year of hospital visits, I relinquished my chaplaincy badge. Unbadged and untitled, I tended to my burnout and trauma.

In rural Taiwan, a return to the humble beginnings of my chaplaincy training. I shadow the wood-carving professor, a spiritual care mayor in her own right, on home hospice visits. Like in Cambodia, the languages I want—Hokkien, Hakka—are beyond my tongue. So, I witness. I feel. I lay a palm on an Amah's rock-hard back as she turns away from her bedridden husband, who moans as the nurse changes his catheter. I understand, the way pain hurts most when it's the ones we love hurting. The Amah's back radiates warmth. When it's time to leave, Amah insists on walking us out. She leans against her cane and waves goodbye. All around her are bodhisattva statues in stone, hand-carved by Agong before his bedbound years.

Because my dad can't bring himself to watch the videotape of his father's funeral, I can't bear to view Yeye's final ceremonial rites either. I can count on one hand the number of times my parents and I talked during my gap year. But Dad, an audiophile who captured my infant babbles on quarter-inch reel-to-reel tapes with a devotion verging on religious, found other ways to speak to me. Before I embarked, he recorded an hourlong recitative of birds, their number and exuberance unparalleled before or since. When I need to weep, I will listen to it again, the way my father's voice quakes when he says my pet name, the way he says *Have a safe trip. Take good care of yourself. This is a recording made in May 2004, in case you forget where is home. . . . It's birds singing, talking, very relaxing. Okay, enjoy it. See you soon,* as if he knows the next time he'll see me is at his only brother's funeral, as if he knows I will need to be called home, even if home is ephemeral as birdsong.

I READ ABOUT A SHANGHAINESE woman my age who has settled in Belgium, where she tries to recreate the flavors of her mother's kitchen. On her weekly calls home to her parents in 上海, she urges them all to keep their videos off. The daughter says she doesn't want to subject Mama and Baba to her uncombed hair and baggy PJs, but the truth is, she's afraid to see 妈妈 and 爸爸's aging faces.

DURING THE DESPONDENCY OF COVID times, a friend in Salt Lake City mourns the death of her longtime companion, that regal feline named for sunshine who cemented our bond. A gray cat starts visiting for long stretches. My friend names the collared pet Persephone: a reminder that she can't stay permanently.*

The plot thickens. My friend suspects there are *two* gray cats, though they never appear side by side. She's pretty sure the latest visitor is Persephone's mother. By month's end, Demeter has adopted my friend.

---

* Also, the cat likes eating grass, and Persephone is the goddess of vegetation.

WHEN I THINK OF HOME I THINK BLANKETS & FUZZY SOCKS
she wrote
& bullwinkle smiled
upon those vibrant patterns of knitted warmth

& entering the ward
of sickness alchemized
into sanctuary whole

i understood my chaplaincy year
on the oncology unit
as a gift of ease
in her final home—

so lasix did not faze
lasix conferred hope
that the socks would fit

though in this familiar abode
i am no chaplain
just a friend—
just a friend we say

while the Upaddha Sutta rejoinders:
admirable friendship is not the half
but the whole of the holy path

WHAT I THINK ARE BOMBS exploding is the lightning storm that sparks the worst fires in recorded California history. One of the fires comes within a mile of my parents' home. Driving back from an off-the-grid cabin in Oregon—their only vacation in all of 2020—my parents will wonder about the charred air and apocalyptic skies.

Housesitting for them the week the fires begin to rage, I am frantic at the prospect of the photo albums going up in flames. I start putting the most important ones in boxes, in case of evacuation. Flipping open the smallest of the albums, I find not photographs but index cards, inked over in a tidy and unfamiliar hand:

86.10.14

预产期过了九天, 小家伙赖在肚子里不肯出来。

My classmates used to gawk when I admitted that I'd never seen my own birth certificate. It was yet another thing that set me apart, like slanty eyes and stinky foods and those funny sticks they eat with, best keep Lassie away from their chinky cleavers . . .

Mom used to say she couldn't remember when I was born, but here it is, recorded in something infinitely better than a birth certificate, the diary of the first year of my life, the missing link connecting me to this world.

11:15出生。是只小胖老虎。

I am nameless the first four days of my life. She calls me kiddo and brat and little fat tiger, until

baba came up with a name: chenxing. registered for the hukou. the beginnings of a little citizen.

Eleven years later, when we visit Mom in Florida, Dad takes me to Epcot, where he chances upon a vendor whom the people around us might mistake for a family member. He pays the man to calligraph my Chinese name on a painting of my zodiac animal. "Daaaaad!" I shriek when I unfurl the poster. "I wasn't born in the year of ox! How can you forget your only child's birth year?!"

I used to bristle at those moments, thinking my truest self was being ignored, forgotten, erased. But my parents had gifted me a blank canvas wide. *You can be more than what you're born into. Stories shape-shift. This one is yours for the writing.*

I READ A PANDEMIC ARTICLE about Asian Americans that doesn't contain the words "China virus" or "anti-Asian violence." It's about how more of us are learning our heritage languages during this baleful season.

I'm learning a dying language and it feels like rebirth. When he finds out about my weekly Shanghainese lessons, Dad stops speaking Mandarin to me. It doesn't matter how 洋泾浜 I sound—he insists on using 上海闲话 as our lingua franca. It's like getting a brand-new dad. Does he get a brand-new daughter as well? Certainly this daughter speaks less and listens more. Asking simple questions is about all I can manage. 掰个是啥人? 侬认得伊哦?

The fires lead to disaster planning, which leads to the photo albums, which lead to questions my dad answers in Shanghainese. More than one of our family members, he speculates, was murdered. *This one embezzled from the Nationalists. Pretty sure this one embezzled from the Communists. Not sure who this is . . .*[*]

My Shanghainese teacher tells me the holidays are blander now. *Who can be bothered to wrap their own 粽子 for 端午节 anymore when it's so easy to go out and buy them? The Shanghai your parents left in 1991 doesn't exist anymore.* I tell her my mom still bothers. Bamboo leaves and sticky rice soaking in her kitchen are the herald of mid-autumn.

In a rare moment of self-disclosure, my teacher mentions that her daughter has just gone off to college. "Far away?" I ask. "No, in Shanghai, but she won't be able to visit because of covid." I feel her sadness tugging on my own, our rivers of grief woven into a common tear-saturated garment. This life schools us in grief, if we are willing to learn, and when we finally spend that currency of connection from our banks, what we reap is—

Oceans of grief and joy tsunami three thousand realms into a single moment. This is not the perfect translation of 一念三千, not the full measure of what the phrase means. *Ichinen sanzen,* living: we can never take the full measure of it, but still, we try.

---

[*] Dazzling and dizzying, the wily unknowability of the past . . .

THE THAI WORD FOR SMOKE sounds like the Thai word for soul.

Please tell me who you are.

—someone who wishes i was better

Thank you. Please tell me who you are.

—someone who wishes i wasn't always wishing i was someone better

Thank you. Please tell me who you are.

—an impossible question to answer

Thank you. Please tell me who you are.

—nothing self, everything kindred

Thank you. Please tell me who you are.

—souls searching in the smoky worlds

Thank you. Please tell me who you are . . .

IT IS 92 DEGREES INSIDE the house and my nostrils are burning from air that smells fried and my eyes are leaking from reading a memoir so brave it breaks my heart, a memoir whose origins are the horror of a sexual assault behind a dumpster, an assault only halted by two Swedish men on bicycles who rushed to the aid of the unconscious woman. I am disgusted that this happened at my alma mater, haunted by the mention of the dumpster, because it must be the same or very nearly the same dumpster that T and I once cycled past, only to be stopped by all the frogs. A whole parking lot covered in baby frogs, no pond in sight. We lay our bikes to gingerly rest. All we can do is stand witness to these asphalt-born creatures and their tiny, determined hops. The precarity of finding our footing in this vast world.

We are broken and healed in more ways than we know.

The autumn we met, that honest season, T invites me to the practice rooms in the music building on campus. We sit on the piano bench in the soundproof booth and recall the class that brought us together. I had only attended the first session; he'd stayed on until the course was canceled due to low enrollment. He tells me the professor has just died, of a brain hemorrhage. We let the truth sink into the silence.

He writes the moment into song: *I will say that I want it all . . . the joy, the pain, the tears, the laughter.*

Pandemic time is like miscooked rice noodles, a clump refusing to differentiate. Except for this strand: every day, for a whole week, a rabbit notices and comes near. We stand at the entrance to the cul-de-sac and wait. It hops out to the sidewalk, sits up on its hind legs, regards us with perked ears, then disappears back into the bushes. After the rabbit no longer emerges, though plunged back into noodle time, fondness's trace remains.

We are each other's bodhisattvas. We are each other's dearest dreams.

IT TOOK GRIEVING OTHER PEOPLE'S stories to learn how to grieve my own. I think of the mercy in the Eritrean uncle's words: *it won't be finished in a day.*

The final blessing from my CPE supervisors was the same benediction my patients had been giving me all year. *Chaplaincy needs writers too.* They spoke what I needed long before I dared to myself.

I am a sparrow on the Phnom Penh riverfront. The cages are gone, the birdseed too. Before and after me: infinite choices, intimate not-knowing.

As a dear friend once wrote:

There is nothing missing in the moments it takes for me to turn over each heirloom tomato at the farmer's market, not just because I'm looking for one to buy, but also because each is unique and lumpy, and bitten, and unexpected. There's nothing missing in admiring the quirky college student making circles on her bike with a giant sunflower hanging out of her backpack. And there is only beauty in taking some time to wonder about the notes this precious old man in glasses across from me is writing in the margins of his book. There's no one there to witness or acknowledge those things, but they're absolutely precious, if only just to ourselves.

There is nothing missing the day a dear friend invites me to a museum exhibit that ignites our pandemic-dulled brains. There is only joy in the hours of outdoor conversation afterward, even if we are cold and masked and about to pee our pants. We are grappling with what it means to be Asian American Buddhist and it feels like chasing that proverbial pot of gold at the end of the rainbow and then we are laughing about "the closure of no closure" and all I can think as she worries a London plane leaf between her fingers is *We are the rainbow. We are golden.*

THE YEAR WE BURY OUR time capsule, that honest fall, this birthday card:

I could go on for ages about how wonderful I think you are & how blessed I feel to have you in my life, & by no means do I question the value of such words—I just know that you understand all of this. And, to be frank, sometimes lots of words just don't quite capture it as well as the simple stuff. I love you. I miss you. I love that so much of you is here. Thank you.

Eleven autumns later, I watch the smoldering sky struggle to clear. *Love?* I whisper to the smoke-choked air. I drive along a forest-encircled stretch of freeway, past the site of my rainbow-formed thirtieth-birthday card, past the turnoff to the open space preserve where I once stood rapt in a silk dress that was and was not meant for me. All I see is a cloak of gray, but they are there, those veiled trees long listening.

I will say that I want it all . . .

AT HER FATHER'S MEMORIAL, SHE addressed an audience of thousands, her voice steady as the faces in the stadium dripped with tears. Others spoke of his contributions to the university, to law and politics, but she told us about her papa who fed the hummingbirds. Now who would make the syrup, fill the feeder? She would, she decided, though the effort of it astonished her. Who knew a waystation for flitting creatures demanded such steadfast upkeep?

At her memorial, I would be among several people to give a eulogy. I closed with my favorite memory of her. Summer 2010, FA Week, Camp Sunshine. At the evening dance party, everyone is dressed up and singing "Don't Stop Believing" to a beloved FA community member in his thirties who has been fighting cancer for several years. Out of nowhere, she tackles me with a bear hug so fierce it knocks the wind out of me, and I know she is grieving how he won't be here to dance with his two daughters next year. And then, with tears streaming down her cheeks, she beams a huge smile—and keeps right on singing and dancing.

IN THE CLOSING SCENE OF *Bangsokol, A Requiem for Cambodia*—after the haunting melodies, after the footage of bombs and forced evacuations and labor camps, after a river of rocks flows to a Buddha altar where photos of the murdered have been painstakingly assembled—after all this, the crocodiles appear. I've heard it's because a crocodile with FOMO once missed a Kathina. The bereft reptile insisted on being represented in banner form at Buddhist festivals thereafter.

Twenty-foot-long spirit flags unfurl onstage, crocodile banners festooned with scales that sparkle emerald, sapphire, ruby, rose quartz. They wave their sequined tails as the musicians begin to ululate and drum, sing and dance. Chaiyam: boisterous music for processions at Buddhist festivals, often with elements of slapstick. The abrupt change of tone jars us to our senses.

After all this, a party? The audience is standing and clapping, white cloths draped around their necks like khata scarves.

In the end, it is this—not the war, not the starvation, not the torture, but the jubilation—that makes me weep.

WHAT I HAVE COME TO LEARN:

    the obstinacy of joy

    the overwhelm of hope

    the crocodiles fly

unglossary

page xvi

胖阿姨 pàng āyí

瘦阿姨 shòu āyí

កើត រ៉ន koet ran

កូន koun

អ្នកគ្រូ neak kru

លោកយាយ lok yeay

page xvii

不知最親切 bùzhī zuì qīnqiè

page 1

一期一會 yīqī yīhuì

page 5

空中飞人 kōngzhōng fēirén

口音 kǒuyīn

page 6

卷舌 juǎnshé

玩儿 wán'r

啥 shá

什么 shénme

傻 shǎ

冰箱 bīngxiāng

page 7

空中飞人 kōngzhōng fēirén

半母语 bànmúyǔ

我要吃饭 wǒ yào chīfàn

我要上厕所 wǒ yào shàngcèsuǒ

文盲 wénmáng

page 8

空中飞人 kōngzhōng fēirén

page 9

空中飞狗 kōngzhōng fēigǒu

page 10

宗教师 zōngjiàoshī

精神支持 jīngshén zhīchí

精神疏导 jīngshén shūdǎo

心理疏导 xīnlǐ shūdǎo

关怀 guānhuái

人文关怀 rénwén guānhuái

心灵关怀 xīnlíng guānhuái

神职人员 shénzhí rényuán

牧师 mùshī

精神与心理关怀 jīngshén yǔ xīnlǐ guānhuái

page 11

你是什麼 nǐ shì shénme

我不是台湾人 wǒ búshì táiwānrén

page 13

白衣觀音 báiyī guānyīn

page 16

在山上 zài shānshang

page 17

姐姐 jiějie

妹妹 mèimei

page 20

拜拜 bàibai

page 21

奶奶 nǎinai

page 23

因緣 yīnyuán

page 25

一期一會 yīqī yīhuì

一 yī

page 26

緣分 yuánfèn

page 27

臨床牧關教育課程 línchuáng mùguān jiàoyù kèchéng

宗教師 zōngjiàoshī

牧師 mùshī

page 28

神職人員 shénzhí rényuán

精神護理 jīngshén hùlǐ

精神支持 jīngshén zhīchí

精神與心理關懷 jīngshén yǔ xīnlǐ guānhuái

心理 xīnlǐ

精神疏導 jīngshén shūdǎo

人文關懷 rénwén guānhuái

心靈關懷 xīnlíng guānhuái

靈性照顧 língxìng zhàogù

page 32

不要问我从哪里来 búyào wèn wǒ cóng nǎli lái

我的故乡在远方 wǒ de gùxiāng zài yuǎnfāng

为什么流浪 wèi shénme liúlàng

流浪远方 liúlàng yuǎnfāng

流浪 liúlàng

为了天空飞翔的小鸟 wèile tiānkōng fēixiáng de xiǎoniǎo

为了山间轻流的小溪 wèile shānjiān qīngliú de xiǎoxī

为了宽阔的草原 wèile kuānkuò de cǎoyuán

流浪远方 liúlàng yuǎnfāng

流浪 liúlàng

还有还有 háiyǒu háiyǒu

为了梦中的橄榄树 wèile mèngzhōng de gǎnlǎnshù

橄榄树 gǎnlǎnshù

三毛 sānmáo

page 37

一期一會 yīqī yīhuì

明天辰星就要出發到柬埔寨了 míngtiān chénxīng jiùyào chūfā dào jiánpǔzhài le

知道她愛貓 zhīdào tā ài māo

在離開前帶她去看最可愛的柚子 zài líkāi qián dài tā qù kān zuì kěài de yòuzi

那被辰星笑稱為青少年的調皮傢伙 nà bèi chénxīng xiàochēngwéi qīngshàonián de tiáopí jiāhuo

趕在我們出店前回來撒嬌 gǎnzài wǒmen chūdiàn qián huílái sājiāo

這個學期辰星和我們一起生活一起學習 zhège xuéqī chénxīng hé wǒmen yīqǐ shēnghuó yīqǐ xuéxí

從大學國文到生命教育研究 cóng dàxué guówén dào shēngmìng jiàoyù yánjiū

也參與到金山醫院的社區安寧與長照關懷 yě cānyù dào jīnshān yīyuàn de shèqū ānníng yǔ chángzhào guānhuái

這位可愛的上海出生美國長大的姑娘 zhèwèi kěài de shànghǎi chūshēng měiguó zhǎngdà de gūniang

帶著靈性關懷師的學習與工作背景 dàizhe língxìng guānhuáishī de xuéxí yǔ gōngzuò bèijǐng

給大家帶來許多的支持與陪伴 gěi dàjiā dàilái xǔduō de zhīchí yǔ péibàn

祝福到柬埔寨之後 zhùfú dào jiánpǔzhài zhīhòu

完成那本書 wánchéng nà běn shū

持續支持需要照顧的人 chíxù zhīchí xūyào zhàogù de rén

page 39

杯弓蛇影 bēigōngshéyǐng

page 40

原諒我 yuánliàng wǒ

ขอประทานโทษ kho prathan thot

សុំអភ័យទោស soum athyeasrai

許してください yurushite kudasai

page 41

雖然很掙扎 suīrán hěn zhēngzhá

但想想還是跟妳說 dàn xiǎngxiang háishi gēnnǐ shuō

柚子在我們上回去吃飯之後沒多久 yòuzi zài wǒmen shànghuí qù chīfàn zhīhòu méiduōjiǔ

因為在外頭玩 yīnwèi zài wàitou wán

不小心吃到老鼠藥 bùxiǎoxīn chīdào láoshǔyào

已經往生了 yǐjīng wǎngshēng le

主人很傷心 zhǔrén hěn shāngxīn

覺得牠在人間時間太短了 juéde tā zài rénjiān shíjiān tàiduǎn le

但我相信柚子能得這麼多人愛 dàn wǒ xiāngxìn yòuzi néng dé zhèmeduō rén ài

一定會去到美好的地方重生 yīdìng huì qùdào méihǎo de dìfāng chóngshēng

page 43

随便聊聊天也可以 suíbiàn liáoliaotiān yě kěyǐ

page 44

心酸 xīnsuān

page 47

媽媽 māma

老師 lǎoshī

奶奶 nǎinai

一路顺风 yīlùshùnfēng

再见 zàijiàn

page 58

菩薩你好 púsà níhǎo

page 61

義工 yìgōng

义工 yìgōng

page 63

龙猫 lóngmāo

page 70

ក្មួនកំព្រា koun kamprea

page 73

成语 chéngyǔ

画蛇添足 huàshétiānzú

楚 chǔ

湖北 húběi

Page 74

画蛇添足 huàshétiānzú

page 78

三个毛豆 sāngè máodòu

page 80

杯弓蛇影 bēigōngshéyǐng

弓 gōng

page 81

半梦半醒 bànmèngbànxǐng

page 83

我睡不着 wǒ shuì bùzháo

page 85

酒鬼 jiǔguǐ

爱人 àiren

盼望 pànwàng

失望 shīwàng

page 94

没头脑 méitóunǎo

不高兴 bùgāoxìng

没头脑和不高兴 méitóunǎo hé bùgāoxìng

page 95

不高兴 bùgāoxìng

没头脑 méitóunǎo

page 96

没头脑 méitóunǎo

不高兴 bùgāoxìng

不要想太多 bùyào xiǎng tàiduō

明天的事情明天再想 míngtiān de shìqing míngtiān zàixiǎng

page 97

韩 hán

page 107

奶奶 nǎinai

大伯伯 dàbóbo

page 115

一路顺风 yīlùshùnfēng

page 120

困难 kùnnan

痛苦 tòngkǔ

失去 shīqù

page 121

外公 wàigōng

page 122

改善 gǎishàn

等死 děngsǐ

page 123

不要管他们 búyào guǎn tāmen

没办法 méibànfǎ

热水袋 rèshuǐdài

page 124

哎呀 āiyā

热水袋 rèshuǐdài

不好意思 bùhǎoyìsi

没什么 méishénme

不要紧 búyàojǐn

你现在身体弱 nǐ xiànzài shēntǐ ruò

应该有人帮你 yīnggāi yǒu rén bāngnǐ

page 125

爷爷 yéye

四川北路 sìchuān běi lù

卢湾区 lúwān qū

困难 kùnnan

痛苦 tòngkǔ

失去 shīqù

明天 míngtiān

后天 hòutiān

天 tiān

星期 xīngqī

月 yuè

年 nián

page 126

回家了 huíjiā le

无家可归 wújiā kěguī

page 129

你已经帮了我很多了 nǐ yǐjīng bāngle wǒ hěnduō le

没办法 méibànfǎ

page 131

奶奶 nǎinai

不要管我 búyào guánwǒ

放心 fàngxīn

舍不得 shěbude

page 132

小菜场 xiǎocàichǎng

没办法 méibànfǎ

我爱你 wǒ ài nǐ

page 134

中國 zhōngguó

page 137

一路顺风 yīlùshùnfēng

贝贝 bèibei

保重 bǎozhòng

走好 zóuhǎo

再见 zàijiàn

page 138

你還好嗎 nǐ háihǎo ma

不久以前她還好好的 bùjiǔ yǐqián tā hái hǎohāo de

page 140

媽媽 māma

放心 fàngxīn

捨不得 shěbude

page 141

謝謝 xièxie

page 142

她二十分鐘前走了 tā èrshí fēnzhōng qián zǒu le

走了 zǒu le

你想她現在在哪裡 nǐ xiǎng tā xiànzài zài nǎli

我們沒有信仰 wǒmen méiyou xìnyǎng

佛教有甚麼想法呢 fójiào yǒu shénme xiángfǎ ne

page 143

謝謝 xièxie

一路順风 yīlùshùnfēng

page 145

不远千里 bùyuǎnqiānlǐ

page 150

還願 huányuàn

page 151

願 yuàn

還 hái/huán

還願 huányuàn

没有母女缘 méiyou múnǚ yuán

page 152

ជំរាបសួរ chumreap suor

សុខសប្បាយទេ sok sabbay te

page 160

韩辰星 hánchénxīng

精神与心理关怀 jīngshén yǔ xīnlǐ guānhuái

page 180

南無本師釋迦牟尼佛 nāmó běnshī shìjiāmóunífó

きんす kinsu

南無觀世音菩薩 nāmó guānshìyīnpúsà

page 183

鼻酸 bísuān

page 185

沧海桑田 cānghǎisāngtián

page 191

一路顺风 yīlùshùnfēng

page 192

田 tián

page 198

大爸爸 dàbàba

大伯伯 dàbóbo / [Shanghainese] du ba[k] ba[k]

page 224

一期一會 yīqī yīhuì / ichi-go ichi-e

page 227

沧海一鳞 cānghǎi yī lín

沧海桑田 cānghǎisāngtián

page 233

一念三千 yīniàn sānqiān / ichinen sanzen

page 234

普通话 pǔtōnghuà

豆腐衣 dòufu yī

豆浆 dòujiāng

灵 líng

灵气 língqì

靈氣 língqì

page 238

阳台 yángtái

page 241

ไหว้ wai

page 242

北京 běijing

[see page 32] 枣子树 zǎozishù

page 243

慈姑 cígū

慈 cí

page 251

ព្រលឹង proleung

ขวัญ khwan

ซอย soi

弄堂 lòngtáng

page 254

上海 shànghǎi

妈妈 māma

爸爸 bàba

page 257

预产期过了九天 yùchǎnqī guòle jiǔtiān

小家伙赖在肚子里不肯出来 xiǎojiāhuo làizài dùzilǐ bùkěn chūlái

出生 chūshēng

是只小胖老虎 shì zhī xiǎopàng láohǔ

page 259

洋泾浜 [Shanghainese] yang jin bang

上海闲话 [Shanghainese] ẓang hɛi ɛi wu

掰个是啥人 [Shanghainese] gaᵏ gaᵏ ẓi sa nin

侬认得伊哦 [Shanghainese] nong nin daᵏ yi va

粽子 [Shanghainese] zong zi

端午节 [Shanghainese] dü wu jieᵏ

一念三千 yīniàn sānqiān / ichinen sanzen

about the author

Photo credit: Lan Le

CHENXING HAN is the author of the widely reviewed *Be the Refuge: Raising the Voices of Asian American Buddhists* (North Atlantic Books, 2021). She is a regular contributor to *Lion's Roar, Tricycle, Buddhadharma,* and other publications, and a frequent speaker and workshop leader at schools, universities, and Buddhist communities across the nation. She has received fellowships from Hedgebrook, Hemera Foundation, the Lenz Foundation, and the Institute of Buddhist Studies.

Chenxing holds a BA from Stanford University and an MA in Buddhist Studies from the Graduate Theological Union. Her chaplaincy training began in Cambodia and continued in the San Francisco Bay Area, where she completed a yearlong residency on an oncology ward. She is a coteacher of Listening to the Buddhists in Our Backyard at Phillips Academy Andover and a co-organizer of May We Gather: A National Buddhist Memorial for Asian American Ancestors.

About North Atlantic Books

North Atlantic Books (NAB) is an independent, nonprofit publisher committed to a bold exploration of the relationships between mind, body, spirit, and nature. Founded in 1974, NAB aims to nurture a holistic view of the arts, sciences, humanities, and healing. To make a donation or to learn more about our books, authors, events, and newsletter, please visit www.northatlanticbooks.com.